ROBIN EMERY

MAINE'S FIRST LADY
OF ROAD RACING

ED RICE

Down East Books

CAMDEN, MAINE

Photography credits: Jack Milton (*Portland Press Herald*/Getty Images), 64, 181; Bill Knight, 130; Hugh Bowden (*Ellsworth American*), 132, 134; Robert Cunningham, 164.

Photographs courtesy of: Robin Emery, 2, 20, 22, 27, 52, 55, 79, 94, 102, 108, 110, 114, 123, 192; Ed Rice, 16, 30, 42, 45, 59, 74, 146, 154, 166, 170,173, 174, 176, 178, 182, 185, 186, 188, 190, 196, 201.

Down East Books

An imprint of The Rowman & Littlefield Publishing Group, Inc.
4501 Forbes Blvd., Ste. 200
Lanham, MD 20706
www.rowman.com

Distributed by NATIONAL BOOK NETWORK

British Library Cataloguing in Publication Information Available

Library of Congress Cataloging-in-Publication Data

Names: Rice, Ed, author.
Title: Robin Emery : Maine's first lady of road racing / Ed Rice.
Description: Camden, Maine : Down East Books, 2019.
Identifiers: LCCN 2018044348 (print) | LCCN 2018047144 (ebook) | ISBN 9781608939046 (Electronic) | ISBN 9781608939039 (cloth : alk. paper)
Subjects: LCSH: Emery, Robin, 1946– | Women runners—Maine—Biography. | Maine—Biography.
Classification: LCC GV1061.15.E46 (ebook) | LCC GV1061.15.E46 R54 2019 (print) | DDC 796.42092 [B] —dc23
LC record available at https://lccn.loc.gov/2018044348

♾™ The paper used in this publication meets the minimum requirements of American National Standard for Information Sciences—Permanence of Paper for Printed Library Materials, ANSI/NISO Z39.48-1992.

Printed in the United States of America

For my father

—Robin

To Susan

—Ed

Contents

Contents

Foreword

I FIRST BECAME "ACQUAINTED" with Robin Emery somewhere early in the second mile of the 1973 Portland Boys Club 5-Mile Race. She just blew past me, a lovely young lady who was a much faster runner than I. She would remain that way (a much faster runner than I) until I passed her, just yards short of the finish line, at the 1980 Grand Willey 10K in Ellsworth.

Yes, it took me seven years to beat her.

And by the time I'd finally reached a finish line before her, I had learned her extraordinary history with road racing in Maine, and I had earned a deep respect for her—before I was fortunate enough to develop a lasting friendship.

In 2012, with such obstacles as a complete left hip replacement and a bulging disc in my lower back (finally operated upon, as a herniated disc, in 2014), I was restricted in my running—but I had an important "obligation" to meet at the Tour du Lac 10-Miler in Bucksport. And nothing could have made my final long-distance Maine race more special to me than to share every step of it, side by side, with Robin Emery.

Our dear friend, the late Fred Merriam, had established a "100-Mile Club," or ten official finishes on the challenging Bucksport course, now recognized by the Maine Running Hall of Fame as one of Maine's truly great, historic races. A hand-lettered poster was displayed each year, with the names of many of my friends, including Robin's, and respected names in the race's history.

In 2011, I had arrived at the race solely to work as a volunteer official. Race director Chris Jones approached me and said, "Ed, did you know that you have nine official finishes?" No, I did not. And it was a damn good thing I didn't have my running togs and racing shoes, even as ill-equipped as I would have been to join those on the starting line.

So, there I was in 2012, to honor Fred's memory and do one last "tour" of a beloved training route (there were memorable ones with Fred and others in the dead of winter, striding carefully through ice and snow, with wind chill factors of minus double-digits!) and racing course.

Almost immediately, Robin and I established a relaxed pace, at the back of the pack, chattering away. We even stopped at the Clappers' home, less than a mile into the race, where our wonderful friends, Charlie and Leona, had put on a postrace potluck luncheon for years and years. We each gave them hugs; they were watching the race from their driveway.

This break wasn't quite so dramatic as when Robin and mutual friend, Skip Howard, stopped en route to a Tour du Lac finish line on a sweltering hot day to jump into Silver Lake (Skip tells this tale in chapter 8), but a very casual tone for the day was set immediately.

Our run together quickly evolved into stories swapped of Races Remembered When We Were Fast. Yes, we acknowledged each and every torturous hill climb that Tour du Lac presents—and then immediately returned to chattering away, on ascents and descents, no matter how measured our breathing became.

Robin has often loved to return to a race course, the day following an event, to "hear the echoes" and now we had an entire race to share hearing such echoes together. Recently, I was so honored when Robin remarked that this event is now a special memory for her; I knew when it was happening how *very special* it was and would forever remain for me (see photo in the afterword).

For years, I have frequently remarked that no member of the Maine running community, past or present, deserves to have a book written about him or her more than Robin. Unfortunately, just as I felt that my running days were well past me, I also thought I was no longer up to the task of publishing.

It was in November of 2016 when my writing and publishing muse returned, for One Last Hurrah. I was listening to my friend, former college professor and New Brunswick historical author Ron Rees, during the book launch for his latest work, *New Brunswick Was His Country*.

And in his introductory remarks, Ron's words struck me like the best possible inspirational dagger anyone could imagine. The subject of his biography, Ron stated simply, "*deserved* to have a book."

Thus, was the shot fired in my race to write and publish a book on the great Robin Emery, a pioneer female runner on the roads of Maine, a stellar performer who set standards of excellence unlikely to be matched or surpassed. And an extraordinary athlete whom I suspect will be, in her own words, "kicking wrinkled butt" and racing in the future as "a very fast ninety-year-old." Yes, "Long May You Run," Robin.

Ed Rice

ONE

Fresh from Tackle Football, All Dirty and with Leaves in Her Hair

WHEN ROBIN EMERY WAS A COLLEGE STUDENT, she came across a book on fitness, decrying the kind of attitude that led to what later generations would refer to as "couch potatoes," using the example of a man who actually used his car to drive to his mailbox. It exhorted people to get up and exercise.

She thought about how, as a child, she'd rebelled from staying in the house to play with dolls and fled outside to play whatever games the boys were playing. And she remembered the frustration she'd known in junior high school and again in high school, with no sports available for girls and only the much-despised "silly dancing" of the cheerleaders as an exercise-activity option.

Now, this fitness author's call to action resonated with her. Doing nothing, she reasoned, meant you were a definite candidate to "clog up."

Recognizing that she should do something, she did. She walked. She walked a lot. She walked "all over the place," both at her school, Allegheny College in Meadville, Pennsylvania, and her parents' summer place, in Lamoine, Maine.

A favorite place to walk was a beautiful, four-and-one-half-mile loop that encircled her home in Lamoine.

"Since I did walk so much, it took a long time to do it," Robin remembers. "The day came when I thought to myself, 'Well, let's just see if I can *run* this whole loop.' So I did. And I made it. It was probably very slow—but," she says playfully, "maybe not. And then I did it the next night. And the next. And—I've never looked back."

Robin remembers wearing an Oxford cloth shirt, Bermuda shorts, and a pair of Docksider shoes for those inaugural runs, hardly anybody's idea, today, of the ideal apparel.

But now, entering her fiftieth year of running, since that first foray in the summer of 1967 as a twenty-year-old, Robin remembers one very vital thing about that particular running experience, "It *feels* good. I'm moving—and it feels sooooo good!"

The young Robin liked to fly, even on her training runs.

Robin Emery was born on October 4, 1946, in Bangor, Maine, delivered by her Uncle Clarence, an obstetrician, who delivered her as well as a number of other Emery cousins. With seven kids in Robin's dad's family alone, relatives were spread around Maine, from Mexico to Bangor to Bar Harbor. Her dad, Gordon, the son of a preacher, was born in Charleston.

Both of her parents attended Edinboro College in Pennsylvania, a teacher's college. And, ultimately, both taught in that state. Her dad taught art. Noting that both her parents got out of school during the Depression, in the 1920s, Robin said it was rare to find an opportunity for an art teacher, but a little town in Pennsylvania, Windber, hired him.

At this time, in Pennsylvania, a husband and wife could not teach in the same town, so her mom, the former Shirley McAllister Simpson, was not a teacher for a while, working in special education and as a teacher's aide. Reflecting on her mother's teaching career, Robin smiles respectfully, "She literally worked her way up through the ranks." After teaching special education, she taught kindergarten, then fourth grade, and ultimately wound up teaching English, for the majority of her career, to juniors in high school. "I used to joke with her that 'One of these days, Mom, you're gonna graduate.'"

Her dad, she remembers, wasn't as much of a student as her mom was "but he could draw anything. His best artistic endeavor was lettering; he could letter anything." He would create beautiful Christmas cards every year with block print cut paper. He liked working in watercolors, doing mostly landscapes, "but he was a perfectionist so I don't have any of his stuff because he threw everything out." Gordon Emery was never satisfied with what he created, and he never really had a studio or anything, Robin recalls. "He taught school, and he taught a lot of kids to draw, students who went on to become artists. He was very well loved in Windber," Robin says proudly.

Though she loved to read, in the early days Robin found math challenging and difficult. It started with a second-grade teacher who "traumatized" her, using Fridays for rapid-fire, timed sessions going over multiplication tables. "I'd get sick every Friday. Mom would send me to school; I'd come home sick. It was horrible. Second grade ruined me for math until high school."

Yes, high school, for more nightmares awaited her in junior high school. By the time she reached seventh grade, in 1957, American education shared the country's hysteria over the Russians putting Sputnik into space and America's desperate need to recover in the space race. And Robin was to discover to her horror, "they'd made THIS seventh-grade class take algebra to keep up with the Russians." She had been moved into an accelerated math class and quickly felt completely overwhelmed. Fortunately, her dad stepped in and had his daughter returned to a more normal setting.

For someone who would make her career, largely working with elementary school students, she knows she learned some important lessons, about what NOT to do, from her own education. It was only well into her high school studies that she finally "realized I'm not stupid." By her senior year in high school, Robin ranked fifth in her class.

As a child, her principal joy was just being outside, playing with the neighborhood boys and being, basically, your classic tomboy. "Boy, my poor mother, how she must have despaired over me," Robin recalls. Everywhere, it seemed to her, she faced conflict. She hated dresses but was expected to wear them to school. And she hated dolls. Here, she tried to make concessions for her mom's sake. She "tried mightily" to play with dolls, for her mom sewed beautiful doll clothes. But, alas, life was not easy for a girl who liked cars, bikes, and trucks. And running.

Robin remembers, "My earliest memories of running, just for fun, would have to be around second or third grade, playing tag and hide-and-seek. Just taking off and running as fast as I could for a few yards and then slowing down. I remember getting out of school and running home so I could get out of my dress—Ugh!—and run some more with my friends. We had a fence in the backyard and I would run down the yard and sail over that fence. What a feeling!"

Today, Robin retains compassion for her mom's plight, "My mom was a lady; she was definitely not a feminist. Still, she didn't think women had to do everything defined as 'female.' I know she was more restricted than I was. She became a teacher, but she also served in the navy during World War II, teaching fighter pilots instrument navigation. So, my mom was a nontraditional woman in some ways. I think she had always wanted to become a doctor, but she couldn't, back in those days. She loved school, but I didn't like it all that well because you had to sit still. I was very difficult.

"All of a sudden we were considered young ladies, not girls. We were told that ladies don't sweat. They can glow, but they don't sweat. And they certainly don't run around a track in their underwear," Robin told George Stevens Academy students, in Blue Hill, in a 1983 speech covered by writer John R. Wiggins for the *Ellsworth American*.

How difficult?

"It was me and the guys, at ages eight, nine, and ten. We'd play tackle football. And the girls would all be saying, in their whiney, little mocking voices, 'YOU're gonna get hurt!' And I'd come home, all dirty, with leaves in my hair with a cheery 'Hi Mom!' greeting," Robin remembers.

And then, up in Maine, Robin found several young boys her age who all came to summer in Lamoine. They grew up together, playing baseball until dark, in a nearby field. Or playing hide and seek, to near exhaustion but unrelenting, until their parents called them all inside. Robin says, "And, yes, I'm the only girl—and I'm playing with the guys, but I don't really know I'm not supposed to be like this. I wasn't treated like a girl by them. I liked baseball, hitting, catching, but especially running. I could always run real fast. I was a skinny little kid, a fast runner, always."

But even then she started hearing "No." It began when the neighborhood boys encouraged Robin to ask a local gardener, who doubled as the coach of the local Little League team, to let her join them on the club. She was around ten years old and she went up to him to ask, only to be rejected. It was very frustrating for her to be told that he wouldn't let her do it. And it would hurt even more when her only sibling, a younger brother four years her junior, Jared, would be allowed to play Little League baseball even though he had, to be kind, *limited* athletic skills.

Going to junior high and high school in Pennsylvania, Robin found there was only football, basketball, and baseball for boys. By the time her brother reached these grades there was track and field, which he participated in; she admits it pained her to see him have these opportunities never afforded her.

It was when she reached junior high school she was to discover that, wait, girls don't do such things. There were no organized sports for girls. Zero. What there was, was cheerleading, which, quite frankly, "looked stupid" to her, "dancing around in costumes." Adults and fellow students asked her to try out but she wasn't interested.

Since her parents enjoyed both tennis and golf, they felt it was possible to find an acceptable sport for young ladies, offering either tennis or golf. Since they were playing more golf than tennis at the time, she chose golf while she was a freshman in high school.

Robin remembers she began playing golf with a horrible, crushing baseball swing but did hit the ball. "I wanted to kill it, like kids do," she recalls. Another issue was her temper. The family played at Kebo Country Club in Bar Harbor and one time, on the tenth hole, Robin lost her temper and launched her club up into one of the huge pine trees adjacent to the fairway, where it remained lodged, well above her. Remembering her father as just the "calmest, nicest man who never raised his voice to me" and would never lay a hand on his children, Robin said her father registered his displeasure with her quietly but very effectively. He and her mother would continue on with their round—but Robin must remain behind until she got her club back down. First she tried using sticks to get it down. When that didn't work, she tried using another club. Subsequently, she wound up getting three more clubs stuck up in the tree, all in the same cluster. Ultimately, throwing a fifth club into them all brought the entire group down.

She says the incident did a lot to help her understand why she needed to harness her temper. And, once her father arranged for a series of golf lessons, Robin found the swing and the game that would ultimately lead her to be one of the finest amateur women players in the state of Maine, carrying an exceptional six handicap at her very best.

Indeed, during the 1970s and early 1980s, Robin Emery was a premier female golfer in Maine. She was women's champion at her home course, Kebo Valley Country Club, Bar Harbor, for three straight years and held the women's course record at 76; ultimately, she lowered that to a 73, just one stroke off the course record set by many-time Maine champion Martha White. The difficult Kebo course, by the way, is where President

William Howard Taft used twenty shots on the seventeenth hole, unable to escape its signature monstrous sand trap. She won the first-ever Mary Jane Golf Tournament at Kebo in 1972 with a 91 and won the Class A-1 gross honors in the State Women's Tournament in her debut, with an 84. She scored as low as a fifth-place finish in the statewide Paul Bunyan Tournament and a fifth-place finish for the top tier of the State Women's Tournament.

So, she had golf. But she still laments not having any sporting activities acceptable for girls at junior high school or high school. "I wanted to be fit but there were not many opportunities open to me," she told students at her George Stevens Academy speech in 1983. "I did take up golf. It is really hard to get out of breath playing golf. It seemed to me the real danger was falling asleep between holes." She was truly frustrated. "You saw the guys playing sports but everyone kept declaring that these were not acceptable for girls. It makes me think of the lyrics in that song that goes: 'You can put your foot in the pool, but you can't take a swim.' All I got to do was play in the band. *Big deal.* But it was something to do. Still, inside, I wanted to get out and run around."

College, for helping to fulfill her athletic desires, turned out no better for Robin. She remembers attending Allegheny College in Meadville, Pennsylvania, majoring in history, with a minor in education. Today, she accepts that her college choice was made more to please her mom than for any other reason. She had applied and been accepted into the University of Maine, which had sports for females.

But after trying out running that four-and-one-half-mile loop in Maine, she returned to college, and continued running on her own there, still in her Docksiders. She remembers being too embarrassed to go into the sports stores and get shoes, except accompanied by her boyfriend, Rick Voelker. That choice turned out badly, very badly, "They killed me. I must have had stress fractures from running in these thin, ballet-like shoes."

Sometimes she'd watch her boyfriend's soccer matches and even there she'd get disapproving looks. "I would watch him from the sidelines, and they wouldn't even let me run and get the ball for them when it went out of play, even though I was the only one watching them as they played in the pouring rain." The reason? "Well, it's because girls don't do that sort of thing," she recalls.

Occasionally there was the rare, different reaction: "One day while I was running in the pouring rain I heard footsteps behind me and all of a sudden I was surrounded by the whole Allegheny cross-country team, all men. No one laughed at me. They thought it was great that I was out there. My attitude began to change," she was quoted as telling George Stevens Academy students in that 1983 speech. Writer John Wiggins went on in that *Ellsworth American* article from her talk: There were no races and no trophies for women in those days. My best reward was a feeling about myself. It was confidence. I also felt a pioneering spirit. I found new limits. I began to go farther. I had no training guide, but I kept going and I have been at it for 18 years, through blizzards, airports and graveyards.

Satisfaction came from just running on her own. And it was while she was in Pennsylvania, at college, that she had that First Truly Memorable run, that one Every Runner can recall because it just feels like "everything is clicking!" Robin says, "I was running down towards the dorm, and it just felt like I'm *flying*!—and that old Simon & Garfunkel song was in my head, you know, 'slow down, you move too fast' and, all of a sudden, that was it for me. I just knew that nothing that feels this good can be that bad for you."

Her mother, however, like so many concerned adults of the era, was troubled. "My mom would say, 'Oh you're gonna hurt yourself, you're gonna do something horrible to yourself.' But people just didn't know. Where females were concerned, the ideas ran wild: 'You're gonna get a moustache. . . . You're not going to be able to have kids.'"

At first she wasn't too pleased with any aspect of her mother's contribution to her upbringing: indeed, she didn't want to believe her mother's heritage was Irish instead of Scottish. But, ultimately, she came to hope that perhaps some aspect of Irish genes could be true: "red hair, green eyes, fast runner!"

Robin does enjoy going down one list: the list of myths from that era about women who dared to play sports. As Wiggins quoted her from that

1983 speech: We were warned that they got muscles; they wouldn't be able to have children; boys wouldn't like you, especially if you won; you would get an enlarged heart, liver, or something, and something horrible would happen to you; you would become a spinster; you would grow a moustache. We were really warned that these things would happen to us if we ran.

One needn't wonder if Robin was running, dreaming about winning races: there weren't any races. She recalls, "I just ran on my own. I ran every day. And it's hard to train your relatives and people because, you know, they're thinking, 'It's raining. What's the matter with you?'"

Ultimately, Robin remembers with pride, "But, pretty soon they don't say 'Do you have to run today?' They say 'When are you going to run today?'"

Robin continued to run, at college in Pennsylvania and at her summer home in Lamoine. Then, she recalls, "It was the last day of college, and it was wicked hot—but I ran, just to get my run in before graduation. And this guy comes up to me and says 'I coach and I'd like to coach you. Can I?' And I said, 'Well, it's a little bit too late. I'm sorry.'"

Robin thinks of another lost opportunity at college: it seems one of the guys in the history department wanted her to go out for the rifle team. Because of her ability at skiing, she thinks it would have been great fun to do the biathlon. Again, thanks to her dad, Robin had begun skiing as a kid, walking up a hill in Pennsylvania on these old skis her dad had found in the garage. They had no edges on them. Robin would ski down the hill and then walk back up. Repeat. Then a kindly teacher took her over to a local skiing facility and helped outfit her with real skis. She immediately developed a lifelong love of skiing.

In sports and the outdoors, Robin found freedom and joyous expression. She struggled with the questioning looks she got from adults, especially those who seemed to telegraph the same, tired, limiting message: "What are you doing? You're only going to have kids. You're only going to grow up to be a housewife."

Fortunately, with her parents, college hadn't been an "if you go" proposition, it had been a "when you go," mandate. But now that she had completed college she was troubled by the severe restrictions she found imposed on females. She remembers, "I became a teacher because I, principally, like helping children, and I like making a difference in a child's life—and, yes, I like the personal lifestyle, with your summers off. Frankly there never really was any other choice for me because you just didn't have much of a choice. You could be a nurse, you could be a secretary, or you could be a teacher; growing up, in my era, those were the choices. And you're going to get married—so I just got into teaching."

She had determined that she wanted to live in Maine "and I didn't care what I had to do. I could wash dishes or whatever." But she feels she got lucky when she got a job at the Moore School in Ellsworth, teaching fifth grade.

It was meeting her parents' expectations on the other score, getting married to Voelker, that was particularly daunting. The rebellious 1960s were happening all around her, but other than wanting to be a girl who did sports, she was, essentially in her own mind, this girl, doing what her parents wanted her to do. "I was totally trying to please them. You've got to do what's right and that included being married," she recalls.

Fortunately, her dad said that she "needed a year by yourself, just to see if you can do it." Robin recalls she had more fun that year than she'd ever had in her life. She had a little apartment in Ellsworth, and it was a year of running, climbing, skiing.

Her dad had been right and right then she knew she didn't want to get married. But her mom "was this snowball: She's getting the dresses. She's taking over. You know moms! My mom took over, and I was too afraid to tell her I don't want to do this—so I got married. We were both too young."

But lest anyone thinks Robin Emery harbors any lingering ill will about what she missed out on from education or from sports, or what she might have done differently if she hadn't made decisions based on pleasing her parents, well, you'd be completely wrong.

Today, you only need to talk to Robin in that family home, long ago winterized for her year-round use, just steps away from her beloved four-and-one-half-mile running loop, and you know Robin only dwells in the past to remember the best of times and to be fueled to succeed by those unhappiest of moments.

"This home," she says lovingly, "has always had a good feeling and everybody, from my family to all our relatives, spent many happy summers here." Many of her aunts, uncles, and cousins would come to Lamoine Saturdays for bean suppers. And the kids would all play outside, while the adults met inside talking and singing. Robin remembers, "I'd play the flute and my mom had a little pump organ."

In 2016 the Emery clan had a family reunion in Lamoine. "And the kids were all out running on the lawn, like we used to do. And we were all in here talking, like our parents used to do. We'd become the 'old people.'"

Tragically, one of those relatives not present was the late Frederick C. "Rick" Emery Jr. Known in the greater Bangor area in the 1950s and 1960s as an outstanding athlete (especially to the author, who regularly struck out on either his fastball or his curve when he pitched Bangor West Side Little League baseball), her cousin Rick fell victim to ALS, or Lou Gehrig's disease, in 2015.

Rick was the son of the well-known and respected physician, Frederick Emery of Bangor. Her Uncle Fred, Robin recalls, was her favorite uncle, one with whom she played golf on occasion.

"Cousin Ricky, back then, was always too cool to come to family things," Robin laughingly recalls, "but he was the apple of my uncle's eye. Uncle Fred loved to go to his games." A star baseball player from Little League right through Bangor High School and Colby College, Rick Emery once played for an elite amateur baseball team called the Comrades. Professionally, after earning his legal degree at Cornell Law School, he worked in the US Attorney's Office for the Western District of New York and, starting in 1989, he returned to Maine as an Assistant US Attorney for the District of Maine in Portland, until his retirement in 2012.

With all this history in mind, Robin considered it a wonderful tribute when her Uncle Fred wrote her, just after her father passed away. "It was this really great letter . . . about how 'you have done a lot for our family in sports,' and 'we're really proud of you.' It was so neat to think that they really noticed."

Over the course of fifty years of running, Robin Emery got "noticed" a lot. But the first ones to do so—well, they *noticed*—and were—stunned!

TWO

Running Scared Until Dick Goodie Delivers "The Talk"

ROBIN EMERY WAS THE EPITOME of the "loneliness of the long-distance runner," for three years, from 1967 through 1969. "I mostly ran at night, in graveyards and places where no one would see me. It was as if I didn't want to be caught running," she remembers.

For someone who has really enjoyed the changing "styles" of running clothes and shoes over the decades, she can laugh today at her original garb. There were bulky sweatshirts and flappy windbreakers. And there were sweatpants or cutoff jeans; sometimes, to "be fancy," there were Bermuda shorts. Wearing blue jeans came with serious consequences because when they got wet "it meant you can't run the next day," sidelined by severe chafing. Finally, the shoes were her boat shoes, which weighed about five pounds apiece and had seams inside, a recipe that spelled blisters—nasty blisters.

But by the early 1970s, she recalls, "I was grudgingly accepted. People waved instead of throwing beer cans at me," she joked, as a guest speaker for a student audience at George Stevens Academy in Blue Hill in 1983 and quoted by John Wiggins in an article for the *Ellsworth American* weekly newspaper.

And it was early in 1970 that she saw a newspaper article announcing an open track competition, with an event for females. This was the Maine Amateur Athletic Union (AAU) Track Meet, with an 880-yard run for women, or one lap around the half-mile, cinder track behind the Garland Street School.

With no opportunities to compete ever in such things as Little League or youth leagues, and with no experience representing a school team in sports ever, this was the twenty-three-year-old Robin's first-ever competition.

She was determined to run. But she had no idea how terrified she'd actually be when confronted with the reality of running in public. And it wasn't a good omen that it was pouring rain.

Her husband, Rick, accompanied her and they went into the school, where she put on a pair of track shoes they'd purchased for the event. "They had big spikes on them, and they didn't fit that well," she remembers.

They went out to the track, only to discover that she was the only one registered to run.

"They dragged two people out of the stands to run with me, to make it an official race," Robin says. "All they had to do was start—and then they dropped out. As I stood at the starting line I was so nervous I could barely move. And when the race started, I took off like a shot, but I just about croaked because I started out way too fast. I didn't *know* anything about it, but I did manage to finish. But then again, I was the only one in the race." As she would be, throughout the 1970s until her divorce, she would be identified as "Robin Voelker."

In 1983, Wiggins quoted her as telling the George Stevens Academy students about this very first race of hers: "I took off as fast as I could, like a kid starting out. Have you ever experienced rigor mortis? Your muscles tie up, because you use up all the oxygen in your blood."

Robin was timed in 2 minutes, 36.8 seconds for the 880. A second, half-mile event for women, held at an AAU track meet in Waterville in 1970, found her the victor in 2 minutes, 24 seconds in "a state record."

In 1970, all that existed, for competitions for women in running, were 880-yard races. Things didn't go much better for Robin when she returned to Bangor for that annual AAU track meet in 1971. She recalls,

"I got out there and saw a female marathoner, and she looked skinny and mean. I was petrified. The gun went off, and my legs wouldn't move. I managed to straggle home in third place."

Something good—very good—however, came out of the experience. The female marathoner's coach, Jeff Johnson, a Massachusetts resident, had watched Robin and approached her after the race. He asked if she'd be interested in having him coach her and send her some training programs. Of course she was interested, and his coaching, plus the racing opportunities he would provide for her, helped immensely over the course of the decade of the 1970s. Johnson was coach of the Liberty Athletic Club, or the Liberty Belles, a track club for women and soon Robin would become a very prominent member of their ranks.

In a follow-up letter Johnson alluded to his talented marathoner-wife, Francie, telling Robin, "We don't train every girl like we do Francie, but the basic principles and philosophy are the same. You're a very talented runner, and if there is anything we can do for you in the way of helping you with your training, getting you to meets, etc., please let us know."

In a feature piece for the *Maine Sunday Telegram* in December of 1976, Robin told Lloyd Ferriss, I was discovered. Then I was running in all kinds of races. I began going out of state. . . . What I do for training is the hard-easy method. I'll begin Sunday doing 14 miles real easy, then I'll run a fast four miles on Monday at a 5:30 pace. Then I'll do an eight-miler the next day and gradually work up to a ten. Hard and easy, mostly on country roads. . . . I've been training so long I sometimes think I see a rut in the road where I've been running all these years. People along my route accept me. Nobody hassles me. Even the dogs are used to me.

Robin diligently trained alone on this road. For someone who'd done a four-mile run on her wedding day, running every day was now a very natural thing for her. As she told Associated Press reporter Jack Aley, "It gives me a headache if I don't run." She was regularly running forty miles a week, to get into shape for 880-competitions, and did a ten-to-fourteen-miler on Sundays "to work up an appetite."

The late Rollie Dyer was a leader in opening the doors to women at the races he created.

Thanks to the forward thinking of individuals like Rollie Dyer and Dick Goodie, who had not only created some annual road races but actively recruited women like Robin and Diane Fournier to come to them, Robin had road races in 1971 to attend and distances far greater than 880 yards to run. With six women in the field, Robin won a 1.4-mile race in Greenville, in 8 minutes, 17 seconds and followed that up by capturing a women's only 10K, in 45:42 in Hollis in May. In June, she attended Goodie's Maine Masters 4.1-mile event in Portland, winning the women's division of the forty-one-member field, in 27:07.

She attended another Goodie event, the Maine Masters/Portland Elks thirteen-mile midi-marathon on October 11, 1971, and had a belated birthday present for herself when she won the women's division in a pouring rainstorm. It was reported that 2.72 inches fell in the Portland area that day. In a forty-six-member field, Robin narrowly beat Diane Fournier, in a time of 1 hour, 37 minutes, 14 seconds, taking thirty-eighth place. Diane, who believes this was the first race where she ever came face to face with Robin (and remains astonished that, on first view, she was munching on a donut!), took fortieth place, in a time of 1:37:30. The legendary Johnny Kelley, two-time winner of the Boston Marathon who ran an incredible total of sixth-one Boston Marathons, took twenty-first place in the Portland race, finishing in a time of 1:23:26.

Diane Fournier told Rick Krause, writing in *New England Running* magazine, July 1984, "I looked at her about two minutes before the race, and she was eating a donut. And I said to her, 'How can you do that to yourself?' She said, 'Oh, I was hungry.' She ran in sweat pants and a windbreaker that was flopping all over the place. She amazed me. She just loped along," Fournier said.

Looking back on their early racing duels, Fournier recalled, "Anything under eight miles Robin would win and anything over eight I would win. Then she started getting better."

Also, in 1971, Robin went to the New England National AAU Cross Country Championships for women, representing the Liberty AC, in Boston, along the Charles River. She didn't place that day, but subsequently ran a 5-minute, 34.6-second one-mile that grabbed Johnson's attention. In a letter to Robin, Johnson wrote that the effort had to be considered "very successful . . . an excellent first attempt." Indeed, he added, "Only four Liberty girls have ever run faster."

The year 1972 became a stellar, historic year for road racing in Maine when the twenty-five-year-old Robin Emery became the first woman to run and cross the finish line (Diane Fournier and Sheila Dodge also ran and completed the course that day) of the Portland Boys Club 5-Mile Race (first held in 1930) in April and became the first woman to run the Bangor Labor Day 5-Mile Race (Maine's second-oldest race, begun in 1963) in September. *[Author's note: Both of these events and Robin Emery's history with both races deserve individual attention and two later chapters give just that.]*

In 2017, Dick Goodie told the author of this book that he stood up for Robin's right to run and Diane's right because, quite simply, "it . . . was . . . time" and it should have happened long, long before that. Robin's ability to run low-six-minute-pace, per mile, without any coaching history or support of any kind made Robin "a phenomenon."

While finding some early success with competition, Robin, nevertheless battled almost debilitating anxiety before races.

Having promoters like Goodie publish pictures of her in local newspapers promoting upcoming races and her attendance there didn't help. Neither did little articles, called "pre-writes" in newspaper parlance, talking about an upcoming race, sometimes identifying the favorites to win.

One such article, by an unnamed writer published in the Portland daily newspapers, announced that Robin was scheduled to appear at the Goodie-created Maine Masters 5K and 10K races, run on the same day in the spring of 1972, which were now to be named to honor the late Rollie Dyer, who had died "in a freak bicycle accident" at the age of thirty. In very sexist but pretty much acceptable-at-the-time language, Robin was called a "twenty-five-year-old housewife" who "upset" Diane Fournier in that rain-soaked Portland thirteen-mile race the previous fall. It falsely concluded of the longtime elementary school teacher, She "daily mixes distance running with a busy domestic schedule." On this very clipping, in her scrapbook, Robin simply penned in ink, "Boo!"

At the Dyer races, Robin won the first-ever women's 10K in 42 minutes, 48 seconds, while Diane Fournier was second. A legendary 1960s–1970s runner in Maine, Bob Hillgrove, remembers having an eyewitness seat to Robin's "historic achievements," seeing her make first appearances but then give record-setting performances both at the Dyer memorial races (1972–1976) and at the Maine Masters–sponsored 5.8-mile event in Cape Elizabeth.

In October of 1972, Ralph Thomas won the thirteen-mile Elks Club race in a record time of 1 hour, 07 minutes, 16 seconds, and Diane Fournier had her measure of revenge over Robin, running 1:26:54, to set a new record for women and finish twenty-ninth overall. Robin took thirty-ninth place overall, in 1:34:31, which also broke the existing women's record.

Again, taking advantage of the opportunity to compete at a higher level for women, out of state, Robin first found that she had to race—herself. Under the watchful eye—for qualification purposes—of well-known Maine AAU official Steve Ross, Robin had to run two miles in less than twelve minutes. She took to a track, alone, and ran a two-miler in 11 minutes, 46 seconds. This qualified her for the 1972 AAU National Championships at Kent State, in Canton, Ohio, in the early summer. In that competition, she placed in the top 10 percent of the field.

The year 1973 unfolded for Robin with a few southern Maine races: on March 19, Robin won the female division (thirteenth overall) of a 10K in Portland, in 41 minutes, 27 seconds, snapping her old record by 1 minute and 21 seconds. In a total field of twenty-six runners, rival Diane Fournier took twentieth place in 46:52. And while Cape Elizabeth native and Northeastern University star runner Larry Greer was capturing the overall title in an eight-mile race in South Portland, Robin was twenty-second overall, winning the women's division over Fournier. At an open four-mile race in Portland, Robin set a new mark for women, with 25-minute, 32-second clocking, breaking Diane Fournier's earlier record, of 28:30, set in 1972.

Again, Robin, her coach, and Dick Goodie all felt that it was important for her to keep taking her show on the road, traveling out of state to meet the best of female competition she could.

In June, she traveled to Boston, to take second place behind the talented Charlotte Lettis at a women's two-mile competition at a sanctioned New

England AAU track and field meet in June. Lettis posted an 11-minute, 13.5-second clocking, with Robin (identified as "Robbie" in the next day's *Boston Globe* account), the runner-up at 12 minutes, 04 seconds.

Still, even with some consistency in racing developing and a few formidable races under her belt, Robin was not able to harness her pre-race nerves. And the days leading up to any competition found her unable to eat and sleep.

"Scared, scared about competing," she remembers. "I had no experiences with it as a kid, or a teenager, or a high school or college student."

Her Waterloo came when her friend, formidable Maine Masters runner Dick Goodie, a World War II veteran and longtime employee of Maine Central Railroad, was driving her to Amherst, Massachusetts. She was to face, among others, Lettis, once again at an AAU track and field championship in a July event. They were in a car, and it all just became too much for Robin to cope with.

"I was a wreck," she recalls. "We're in the car and I was almost sick. I never had done sports and I never had to deal with nerves. And that's probably why I was so fast. There was all this churning going on."

Diane Fournier, Dick Goodie, and Robin, at a race in the early 1970s

Goodie determined it was time—for—The Talk.

Able to laugh about it now, Robin soberly heard him loud and clear as he said to her, "'Nobody goes to jail if you come in second. Your mother is still going to love you. Your father is still going to love you. And everyone else is still going to like you. . . . I will like you.' . . . And ever since then I see, he's right."

Today, whenever she encounters another runner suffering from similar anxiety issues, like Ellsworth's Suzy Fay, she is quick to pass along the important advice she first heard from Dick Goodie on a tumultuous car ride to Amherst, Massachusetts. Robin took second place in her event at the Amherst AAU meet. "It's kind of counterproductive when you're so scared you can't even move," she notes wryly.

Experience, in all kinds of racing events, was helping. In the heat of the summer, while Ken Flanders was winning a 6.6-mile race in South Portland, Robin, as the sole female, finished in thirty-third place, in a time of 50 minutes. In a field of fifty runners to start, the extreme heat caused fourteen men to drop out. A talented, blind runner named Joe Pardo, using a cane, took twenty-third place in a time of 46 minutes, 40 seconds.

In the fall, Robin took second in an all-female New England Cross Country 3K race at the Clauson's Golf Club, in Falmouth, Massachusetts, finishing just seven seconds behind the winner. She beat the New England female two-mile champion, Sara Mae Berman, who was third.

And at the annual, fall Portland Elks thirteen-mile Midi-marathon, Ralph Thomas won again, and Diane Fournier won the women's division again, in 1 hour, 27 minutes, 47 seconds, with Robin, in second, in 1:30:12.

On May 19, 1974, Robin participated in a women's 10,000-meter national championship at Central Park in New York City. The first-place winner, Marlene Harewicz, broke the established world record for women at the distance, with a 35-minute, 31-second clocking. Well-known women's distance runner Nina Kuscik took fourth and Robin was fifth, in a time of 40 minutes, 30 seconds, in a very elite field.

Robin ran her first race outside of Maine, at the 1973 New England Cross Championships, in Boston's Franklin Park, where she took 5th place.

By 1975, Robin was registering victories and quality races at all the usual, annual races. Robin won the 1975 Dyer 10K race, taking sixteenth place overall, in new record of 37 minutes, 51 seconds (her old mark was 40:31). Future Olympic champion Joan Benoit won the 5K in 19:20.

In a 2015 feature article written for the *Ellsworth American*, Taylor Vortherms quoted the then-fifty-seven-year-old Joan Benoit Samuelson as remembering, "Robin was a live wire. She exuded excitement and joy for the sport."

Benoit Samuelson recalled, according to Vortherms, how Emery would playfully attempt to psych her at the starting line, interrogating her about whether she was ready for the challenge of "being tested that day."

Vortherms humorously stated, "Emery denies this. Sort of." Dripping with playful sarcasm, Emery responded, "Me? *Me*? No—I *never* did that."

The journalist then quoted Emery enacting her version of the age-old game of playing head-games with a respected rival, "Joanie, you look like you have a limp. Are you OK?" And, of course, Robin snickered and laughed.

Robin told Vortherms, "Joanie was funny—she'd start at the back of the pack and work her way up. You didn't even know she was there sometimes until she'd pass you."

After Robin had taken a fourth straight Portland Boys Club race, columnist Vern Putney, writing in his usual, old-fashioned-gentlemanly style often coupled with a bit of hyperbole, said that, at age twenty-eight, her evolution as a champion runner was "coming like last week's winds. Maine's queen race bee appears to float like a feather. By comparison, Muhammad Ali moves like a dray horse." He continued, "Of course, a lissome lass lugging only 123 pounds on a 5-7 frame makes for easy striding."

Of her diet concerns, Putney noted that, "At race's end, she relaxes with a Coke. She shuns special diet, but is partial to pasta the night before a race. 'It's said to be high in carbohydrates,' she explained to Jim Carroll, who at 64 sought out this slip of a girl for training advice," wrote Putney.

In another interview, Putney asked the always personable, accommodating Robin what she did mentally to handle running alone in harsh elements, like rain, wind, and snow. Robin told him, "No problem. I admit to singing in the rain to pass the time. When I'm shooting for a six-minute race, I switch mental gears to 'Baby Driver,'" a Simon & Garfunkel song enjoyed by those who like folk rock. "It has an upbeat, six minutes per mile running rhythm." She continued, "When I'm in competition, I chase the blues out of my mind and frame a sign in big capital letters–GO."

The real highlight of her 1975 season—and, indeed, a highlight of her entire running career—came when Robin returned to New York City's

Central Park on May 10, 1975, where she finished seventh, but in an excellent time of 37 minutes, 41 seconds, in the 10,000-meter (6.2-mile) Central Park race for women.

In an article published in the Portland newspapers prior to the event, Robin told columnist Putney that she wanted to improve her performance over her participation in the event the year before, even though the actual "national championship" in 1974 had been held in California. Most the class contenders, she told Putney, resided in the East, with Harewicz coming from New Jersey. Jackie Hansen, second place finisher in 1974, was from California, but then came two Long Island, New York, residents, Martha Greene and Kuscik. The key, Robin told the writer, was that the year before she "paid the price for nervousness and inability to eat for two days."

She was even able to tell Putney that she was "no longer in awe of racers' reputations." There was demonstrable evidence: she'd improved on her Dyer Memorial 10K Riverside Course, running 37 minutes, 51 seconds and lowering her previous best mark by 2 minutes, 40 seconds. Then she improved her time at Portland Boys Club 5-Miler with a 29:10 time, almost two full minutes better than her own record pace from the last year.

The Riverside course, Robin told Putney, "is far tougher on the legs and the clock than Central Park's gentle slopes." From her 1972 Dyer 10K time, which was 42 minutes, 32 seconds, she now owned that 37:51 personal best.

Thus, it a far more confident Robin Emery traveled to New York City and ran a competitive race in a stellar field.

It was a field of 310 women, many of them nationally ranked; it was later billed as "the largest ever" for women. The winner, Charlotte Lettis, ran 35 minutes, 56 seconds. Robin was pleased with her time because it was more than two minutes faster than she'd done the previous year at the race. She said, "I've been running sixty miles per week for three years and I guess it's finally paying off."

Joan Benoit, then a high school senior, ran twelfth at this race, in 38 minutes, 03 seconds. Robin told Putney that she was "pleased to beat noted national runners like Nina Kuscik, Anita Scandurr, and Kathy Switzer." Benoit called it the best race of her career to that point.

Robin was "sponsored" at the race by Charles Katsiaficas, who coached Ellsworth High to Maine schoolboy basketball championships in 1953 and 1954, was in the real estate business, and later became famous as a long-respected schoolboy basketball official.

An interesting political note was struck loud and clear from the New York City competition when it was reported that "women were upset" by the notion that a 6.2-mile race for women was being termed "a mini-marathon." A protester, a New York gentleman, wrote and said such a term "denigrates" women.

In the fall, back in Maine, Robin made the rounds again.

In October 1975, she finished second to the elite runner Lettis, who ran 1 hour, 18 minutes, 07 seconds, for a new women's record, at the thirteen-mile Portland Elks Midi-Marathon and finished sixteenth overall. Robin was second, in a time 1:23:05, for twenty-sixth overall, but, more importantly, with a new personal record for her.

And in November 1975, Robin finished twenty-fifth at the Cape Elizabeth 5.8-mile Turkey Trot, in a time of 35 minutes, 46 seconds, to win the event.

As her 1976 racing season got untracked, Robin continued to improve upon her times. On March 27, Robin beat Joan Benoit in the Dyer Memorial 10K, racing at six-minute pace right from the start, opening up a quick fifty-yard lead. She posted a new record, of 37 minutes, 26 seconds, improving 25 seconds from her performance the year before. And at a July 24 event called the Bernie's Fashions 2-mile run, Robin bested a field of thirty-five women, to win, wire-to-wire, in 11 minutes, 55 seconds.

In early July, she told *Bangor Daily News* reporter Bob Haskell, in her very direct, honest way, about why she was traveling out of state to attempt to improve: "You must be noticed by someone from out of state and you have to leave Maine to find good competition among women," she said, identified by Haskell as the "outspoken" twenty-nine-year-old, now six years into her career, and coached by out-of-stater, Jeff Johnson of Massachusetts.

Haskell noted that Robin was representing the Seacoast Striders. "She's 120 pounds, averages 6-minute pace, likes the distance between 5 and 6 miles," and had done a longest-run-ever of fourteen miles. He added she was "thinking about" doing a marathon.

She would top the longest distance that fall, when she ran a fifteen-miler in Charleston, West Virginia, on September 4, in a time of 1 hour, 50 minutes, 02 seconds. She would later tell Portland newspaper writer Lloyd Ferris, in the mid-1980s, that "The most fantastic race I ever entered was in Charleston, West Virginia. A thousand of us lined up on one street and when Jesse Owens fired the gun we raced out of the city and up a mountain in a column a mile and a half long. I can't describe the feeling, that feeling of elation."

She did also note the following: "When I was racing in West Virginia this year I had five guys sprint by me at the finish line. They looked as though they were dying. I think they didn't want to be beaten by a girl. But mostly I don't find that hostility."

Back on the roads in Maine, Robin was to discover that she was having a special influence on some young women joining the road racing scene. One such individual was Kim Moody (known as Kim "Beaulieu" during much of this period): My first race was in 1977, while I was a nursing student at Westbrook College. I placed and Robin won. We spoke afterwards; she was so enthusiastic to learn that this was my first race, and I remember finding her authentically interested in me as a twenty-two-year-old, about my life and my new interest in running. I was really excited to learn about her, her teaching career and her running career. She encouraged me to keep racing and, of course, I did.

Kim continues, "Robin was truly an amazing pioneer for women's running and racing in Maine. I always looked forward to seeing her at the races. Robin was and is such an inspiration to many!"

It was 1977—more than a decade since a young girl had begun running a lonely coastal Maine route of four and one-half miles, just to see if she could do it. Now, she'd not only been instrumental in opening the doors to females to run, but she'd established records at races all over her home state that might never be matched.

Robin was frequently a blur to her fellow competitors. Here, at a race in the early 1970s, her dad captured this image of her, literally flying through the air.

The cherry to sit atop this sundae, representing a decade of excellence, came when she read in *Runner's World* magazine about a race in Johnstown, Pennsylvania, close to the high school and the college where she'd never been given a chance to compete or even participate in athletics. She told her dad about it, and since he was interested in traveling back to see friends in the area where he'd taught for so many years, both father and daughter agreed they'd like to go. Gordon Emery went down first and then, when Robin finished teaching her school year, she flew down to meet him.

"It was so cool to run a race in a place that never offered sports to me when I was a kid. It rained, but I won and I got a trophy, with a female figure on its top, in a place where I was never allowed to do anything," she recalls.

Robin won the race in a time of 37 minutes, 54 seconds. The second-place finisher was well behind, in 40 minutes, 10 seconds.

"It felt *awesome*—to go back to that place where there were no sports for girls and say, 'So there!' and, yes, I still have *that* trophy," she says.

THREE

Diane Fournier Joins Robin in Breaking Down Barriers

ROBIN EMERY AND DIANE FOURNIER seem to have little in common, when you consider their ethnic and cultural backgrounds, but, when you compare their athletic biographies, they have a great deal in common, especially when you consider their innate desire to go where girls weren't supposed to want to go, aided by compassionate, supportive fathers.

So, when they saw each other, shortly before the start of the 1972 Portland Boys Club Race, neither young woman was interested in raising any feminist banners to scream out about how they were the first to break down barriers; they just wanted to run.

Where Robin had first been enticed to want to run, rather than walk, the four-and-one-half-mile loop near her home in Lamoine, the athletic challenge that had been Diane's personal siren was Worthley Pond in Peru. It was about thirteen miles from her Rumford home; she wondered if she could swim the whole length of, up and back, a distance of around three miles. Later, when she became a runner she would run to, or run back from, this same pond.

As a kid growing up, she'd actually been afraid to swim. Later, as an eighteen-year-old senior in high school, she thought of herself as a good swimmer. At the time she'd regularly swim across the wide part of it, a one-half-mile swim. She felt ready for a larger challenge. Ah, but there was the little matter of—black water!

Her dad would occasionally take her water skiing on the pond, but whenever he and the boat passed through black water, or a section of the pond where Diane could not see the bottom, she hated it and was rapidly developing a major phobia. Water skiing *across* black water was one thing but actually swimming *in it* terrified her.

One day, when she was a high school sophomore, Diane remembers, they were out water skiing, and her dad had circled into a black water section when—suddenly—the boat died. Diane recalls, with a wide smile, that her father called back "Oh, we must have run out of gas," and Diane was left to tread water right in the midst of her worst nightmare. Only, of course, to discover there was nothing to really fear. It was then that her father started the boat back up again—*Surprise!*—and father and daughter resumed the water skiing outing.

Then, in her senior year in high school, Diane could not let go of the idea that she should try to swim the 1.5-mile length of the pond and then swim all the way back, for all three miles "just to see if I could do it." She mentioned the idea to her dad and he, very matter-of-factly, said he thought she should try. Diane admitted to him that she was afraid to do this, all by herself. And he quickly responded that she wouldn't be alone: he'd be there, right with her, all the way, in the boat alongside of her. And that's just how Diane and her dad, Arthur R. Fournier, a paper mill worker by trade and part-time groundskeeper, completed Diane's big swim adventure in Worthley Pond.

Diane was an only child, born on November 22, 1946. "I think my dad had wanted a son but he taught me everything I knew about sports and he was my biggest person cheering me on," she says reverently. Because of him and his early influence, Diane believes, she never got caught up in all the fuss about females participating in this sport or that sport. "There were a lot of things I didn't think about. I just thought it was normal, and I owe that to my dad."

So, this was how Arthur Fournier, who never did high school sports himself but was a speed skater of note ("Many people used to like to tell me how good he was," Diane says proudly), came to be his sole child's role model for doing sports. Sadly, because of World War II, he never got to pursue his talents as a speed skater; however, later he impressed his

Diane Fournier, with furry friend, early 1980s

daughter with his ability at swimming and water skiing. And when he learned to snow ski in his late thirties, he was very good at that. "I liked skiing with him because he did ski fast and showed me no mercy," Diane recalls, laughing.

When one asks Diane if she felt remarkable for being a girl and being so athletic, she says, quite matter-of-factly, that she and her dad "never saw what we were doing as anything special. What's different about me skiing or me running—versus some guy skiing, or some guy running? My dad was only reinforcing this idea in my head."

Her father coached the high school ski team and since, Diane remembers, "I was the best skier on the team, it was kinda tough because of the father-daughter relationship. Once, it was funny to me when my father made the discovery that 'girls cry a lot.' But I never cried. Even when I got hurt. And my father was always so supportive. He'd say to me, 'You know, you can do anything you want. Who says you can't?' and there were times he'd tell me 'I don't think you've reached your potential.'"

Whether it was swimming, skiing, or ski jumping, and, later, running, it simply wasn't a big deal to her to be the *only* woman competing. Again, very matter-of-factly, she says of those moments, "You know, I never noticed."

She says "being the only girl" began pretty young when she started Alpine skiing (downhill). She followed her cousin, Sonny, around, doing sports with the boys, "doing things that would have given my grandmother a hemorrhage." Her father picked up on this factor when she began skiing with the high school team. "He always made sure I skied with guys. Guys never stopped, like girls did. No offense, ladies—but we'd go, top to bottom, top to bottom. I think because I did a lot of stuff with boys, it was never a problem."

In all athletic endeavors, quite simply, "my dad always encouraged me to do my best. I was a shortstop when I played softball. And that was because of my dad, because he would work with me, all of the time." For instance, when her ski racing was improving to the point where outside competition could make a difference, "my dad would work 11:00 at night to 7:00 in the morning—and then we'd drive to Vermont, for a race for me to compete in."

And ski *jumping*? Rumford had a tower that wasn't a natural jump site and included a knoll that had to be cleared as an additional obstacle. "Frankly," Diane remembers, "it was very scary, but I told my father I wanted to try it." Once she was at the top, she thought to herself, "Do I really want to do this?" And then he told her it was all-clear at the bottom, which was pretty obvious, since it was just the two of them. "I started down, but I dragged my hands. I did not have enough speed. Both my skis ejected—and that should have been the end of that. So my dad said, 'We're going home.' And I said, 'No.'" So, Diane says, she went back up to the top, didn't drag her hands—and cleared the knoll. She was twelve or thirteen years old at the time. And, she notes, even if she had hurt herself, she'd have never admitted it. Why? "You don't want your mom to know!" she concludes.

How did her mother feel about all these sports? "My mother was *not* a sports person." Did she have to be "a girl" for her mother? "Well, when I was quite young, she tried to have me do 'girl things' like mothers do." She got Diane some dolls. "And my dad said to her, 'What would you like her to do with those?' It hurt my mother that I wasn't big on dolls, but she came to accept it. There were certain things she never understood. She never understood ski jumping. 'That's a boys' sport,' she'd say to me. And I'd respond, 'Who says?' It was a lark, something to do, an athletic challenge."

Running first came into the picture for Diane to get into shape for skiing. She became an avid skier in both cross-country and Alpine, competing in college in Alpine at Western State College in Gunnison, Colorado. Fournier, who was five foot two and 118 pounds, had been training as a cross-country skier, biking and running five to ten miles a day.

Unlike skiing, there weren't any races and it never occurred to her to consider road racing; until the Boston Marathon of 1970, women were still not permitted to participate in the historic event.

Because of an edict going all the way back to the 1920s when a few female competitors, vying for medals and hoping to prove they were the best in the world, had shown extreme fatigue, grown faint, and even fallen to the ground after completing a middle-distance event at the 1924 Olympics, the Amateur Athletic Union (AAU) had declared women "physiologically incapable" of running any distance over five kilometers (3.1 miles).

When long-distance runner Roberta "Bobbi" Gibb discovered she could not receive an official entrant number to participate in the 1966 Boston Marathon, the local Winchester, Massachusetts woman asked for an explanation. Told about the AAU mandate that the Boston Athletic Association (BAA) was accepting, Gibb determined that she must run the marathon and prove how completely misguided and wrong the perception was. Gibb completed the 1966 Boston Marathon in 3 hours, 21 minutes, besting two-thirds of the male entrants to the finish line. Gibb returned in 1967 and again in 1968, and she completed the whole distance; today, Bobbi Gibb is accepted as the "women's division winner" for the years 1966, 1967, and 1968. Gibb was being joined by other women, too, willing to defy the AAU and the BAA by running and completing the marathon. But now BAA officials were actually blocking the finish line, not allowing people without official numbers to cross.

Through cross-country skiing Diane had come to know Sarah Mae Berman and, once while staying at Berman's place in New Hampshire,

Berman enticed her to run the 1970 Boston Marathon. Not at all fond of large crowds and bothered by the stares she was receiving, Diane remembers, "I got there—and looked around—and wondered to myself, 'What the heck am I doing here?' and Nina Kucsik [another of the legendary pioneer female runners] came up to me and asked who I was. I told her that Sarah Mae Berman had told me I should come run this. And she said, 'They're probably going to try to kick you out. So, if they do—run down the sidewalk, for about a mile, and then get back into the race.' Well, there were these two guys in front of me; they're about as wide as they are tall. And they turned around and, said, 'Don't worry. We'll take care of you, honey.' They were from Ohio." In all, there were twelve women who ran 1970 race, in defiance of Jock Semple and the other BAA officials. Diane says she ran the marathon in 3 hours, 58 minutes—and still hasn't forgotten that 1970 was also the year Gatorade came out and was available at Boston's water stops. "It was so salty. I almost threw up."

Back in Maine, in the early 1970s, two very special men helped facilitate interest in road racing in southern Maine by creating annual races to entice *both* males and females into recreational running: Dick Goodie of Portland and the late Roland Dyer of Winslow. According to Goodie's colorful book of reflective essays about road racing in Maine, called *The Maine Quality of Running*, published in 1984, it is thanks to inspiration like Dyer's that road races in Maine increased from twelve in 1966 to forty-seven in 1971.

And, at about that same time, coach Jeff Johnson, representing the Liberty Track Club for females exclusively, reached out to Robin Emery to join (becoming Robin's very first coach); he also contacted Diane, sending her a letter asking if she'd be interested in joining the team and representing it in marathons. He'd become aware that Diane had already run the Boston Marathon. Johnson gave Diane her first uniform. And although she never actually went to competitions on behalf of the club, whenever "anyone asked me who I ran for, I'd say Liberty—because that's what the jersey said."

It was nice to have a jersey designed for running because nothing Diane wore in these early days was specifically designed for women to run in. Diane recounts that her earliest training outfit included "a regular pair of shorts, which gave you diaper rash, and a cotton turtleneck, that won't keep you warm and will be a problem if it gets wet, and a pair of shoes that can only be considered minimalist [basically, providing no arch support, or support of any kind]. They had a little rubber sole and there was no thickness to them." Asked if they ever wore running shoes for boys, she responds, "Oh yeah, there were no shoes for women."

Through connections like Goodie and Jeff Johnson, Diane believes, Rollie Dyer invited Diane to participate in a nine-mile race, using a basic three-mile loop he was putting on in Winslow. It was her first Maine road race. Dyer, who tragically died in a bike accident in 1971, is someone Diane simply terms "a very special person." She states, "He loved the sport, and he was like the younger version of Dick Goodie. He wanted to make sure you had a bathroom to use, a place to change, and would always profusely thank you for showing up at the race. I never got the impression we (female runners) were there as like an ornament. He just genuinely liked to have you there." Dyer, she added, even "made sure that I had a trophy that had a female figure."

Dyer "made me feel accepted," Fournier said. But there were a few other women running in the summer of 1970. The results in Roland Dyer's road racing newsletter, the *Pine Tree Road Runner*, indicate that Fournier won a women's mile run in Gardiner on May 10, beating the only other female competitor, Nancy Gillespie. Fournier was timed in 6 minutes, 11 seconds, and Gillespie, in 6 minutes, 58 seconds. In early August in a 1.5-mile race for women in Winthrop, Fournier topped a field of four women with a time of 9 minutes, 31 seconds. Christine Cos took second, with Patty Rosen, third, and Janice Roberts, fourth.

And then Dick Goodie had Diane Fournier's name. "After that, I was always being invited to these races," she says, laughing. She recalls, at the outset, these inaugural annual events "would attract fifteen, twenty, twenty-five people—but that was a big crowd back then. A nice part of this is that you got to know everybody."

One such race was the 1970 Portland Elks thirteen-miler, for which she has one very amusing memory. "It was a windy day, and I was behind these two big guys, and they were breaking the wind for me. They got upset with that. And, at one point, they complained. 'Why are you behind us? You're ready to run in front of us.' And I said, 'Well, why should I?' Then I went ahead and beat them to the finish line. After, I went up to them and thanked them, acknowledging that they kept me going." They all parted on amicable terms.

In 1971 Diane ran the Boston Marathon "illegally" once again. It would be her last Boston Marathon but, ironically, it was also the last year Boston was off-limits for women; in 1972 BAA officials opened the race to women and began celebrating female champions and age-group winners.

It came about this way: early in 1971, she began training with Mike Gallagher, who was the US national cross-country ski coach, a respected name in the sport all over America. They were both at Springfield College, doing graduate school work and in the same statistics class. Gallagher and a group of men would regularly train together and, Diane remembers, smiling at this memory, "I tried to run with them, but I was always in the back. And it got to be the same deal for me: the guys would be out front—but the dogs wouldn't bark at them, they'd bark at me. I was always bringing up the rear."

It was then that Gallagher said to her, "Let's go run Boston." And she responded, "Sure."

That year it was forty-two degrees and rained the whole way, with legendary English runner Ron Hill winning it. As an official entrant, the cold and wet Gallagher crossed the finish line, was given a blanket and escorted into the Prudential Garage, out of the elements. When the equally cold and wet Diane Fournier came down Boylston Street toward the finish line, she had to veer off the course, denied the opportunity to cross the finish line. "Well, I was fortunate Gallagher's mother had something to cover me with. At least I had a ride home," she recalls stoically.

Had she worried about being detained on the course? "It wasn't so bad that year. But I was careful anyway. I made sure I hung back, and that I was with a number of people. It seemed to me like a huge number of people, especially not knowing anyone, especially compared with the twenty-five people in the road races in Maine!" she remembers.

What have her experiences running the historic Boston Marathon meant to her? "Frankly, I was clueless. But there were three things that made a huge impression upon me. First, the crowd cheering you on regardless—then, secondly, coming through Wellesley [where the all-female Wellesley College population traditionally cheers wildly]. The guys are saying, 'I'm glad I'm running with you—because I feel like I'm being cheered.' Then coming down Boylston Street, coming down to the end—and looking at the finish—and wishing I could cross." As for her time, Diane believes she had a better race than the previous year, estimating her finish time at around 3 hours, 40 minutes.

By 1972, Maine still only had a couple of continuing road races, attracting solely men for the most part. "Running," Diane says, "hasn't caught on with women. It's still in the dark ages." She does credit Dick Goodie for all he was doing to put races on in southern Maine—and invite women. And, Diane firmly believes, it was also helpful when people saw her name, Robin's name, and the names of the other females who did come out in the early 1970s in the race results sections of Maine newspapers.

But 1972 would prove to be a defining year for women running roads, not only at the Boston Marathon—but at the oldest continuing road race in the country outside of the Boston Marathon: the Portland, Maine Boys Club 5-Mile Race, which first began in 1930 and, traditionally, is held on the same day as the Boston Marathon, on Patriots' Day (the third Monday in April, a state holiday in both Massachusetts and Maine). There was no record of any woman ever participating prior to that year. The reason: comparable to the Boston Marathon, admission—to men only—was made by preregistration.

On behalf of both Robin and Diane, Dick Goodie wrote a letter to the Portland Boys Club race officials seeking admittance into the race for them. Diane says she doesn't know what was in the letter but that it essentially said, "We had been in races. This wasn't a lark kind of thing. We'd trained. And we didn't see why we couldn't be there."

While the brief heart-rate exam Boys Club officials required of participants before the race did not upset or even phase Robin in the least, it infuriated Diane and she flat-out refused to participate. "I didn't think I needed to take a physical. I thought that it was invasive. I don't even know why the guys had to do it. . . . And that's when my hackles went up," she states. "I was thinking to myself, 'Why do I have to do *this*? I run every day, and I haven't died yet.'" Still, clearly irritated at the thought of the exam today, Diane adds, "I was so mad that they said I had to have it. But I ended up not having it. I didn't put up much of a stink either."

Outside, milling around in front of the Boys Club Building in downtown Portland, a good-sized crowd had gathered for the start of the race, probably aided because of publicity about women entering the race. Diane was already aware of Robin, most likely from hearing Dick Goodie talk about her. Since Diane already knew a lot of the men running at that time, she was exchanging pleasantries and everything was quite cordial. "And then I saw Robin—" Diane says, smiling broadly.

But what blurs her memory about this sighting and others that occurred frequently that very year was what Robin might—or might not—have been doing at this particular starting line that *always* horrified Diane every time she did see her do it.

"So, I see Robin—and she was probably eating a donut before going to the starting line! I'm the kind of person who has trouble eating a meal well before a marathon and now I'd see her do *this* again and again—and it would all but make me sick watching her. Sometimes she'd say to me, 'Want to take a bite?' and I'd pull back and say, 'Noooo!'"

In their first head-to-head competition, Robin came in first, in a time of 33 minutes, 04 seconds. Did Diane see her? Acknowledging her better rival that day, Diane says, "I saw the backside of her. And since she's tall, compared to me, that also made it a little easier to spot her." Just as it is a lasting memory for Robin, Diane, too, was startled by the reactions of people all along the five-mile route. "You heard people saying, 'Oh there's a woman!' And then they'd see me, and say, 'There's another woman!'"

According to Dick Goodie's book, a third woman, named Sheila Dodge, participated in the 1972 Portland Boys Club Race, but neither Robin nor Diane saw her. Goodie's book is a treasure trove of results from Maine's earliest, continuing road races, carrying results through 1983, and listing the first three finishers in both the men's and women's divisions.

Robin Emery won a total of nine Portland Boys Club races, including four straight times, from 1972 to 1975, and then an additional four more straight times, from 1980 to 1983. A ninth win came in 1985. Robin set her personal record (PR) on the five-mile course of 29 minutes, 06 seconds in 1981. Diane Fournier would only return to the Boys Club Race one more time, in 1974, when she finished second to Robin.

The third-place finisher in the women's division in 1974 was a schoolgirl—named Joan Benoit; Benoit would finish second to Robin at the race in 1975. Signaling loud and clear that she would be something extraordinary on the roads, Joan Benoit won the Boys Club race in 1976 and, of course, went on to make both a national and international name for herself, winning two Boston Marathons (1979, and, in world record time for women, 1983) and the first-ever women's marathon in the Olympic Games of 1984.

When Diane saw Joanie at the 1974 Boys Club race, in the spring of the year, she was well into her first year teaching and coaching one sport at Mt. Ararat High School. She remembered seeing the young Benoit girl, representing Cape Elizabeth High School, win the one-mile race at an all-comers from all-classes A-B-C-D meet ("A" for the largest enrollment schools down to "D" for the smallest). Girls could only run the one-mile at that time. "I remembered her from that meet. And she talked to me a little about her victory. We've chit-chatted from time to time ever since." Diane pauses, adding, "She's such a great person," laughing at the memory of her most recent meeting with Maine's most famous athlete of all time: "We were in a grocery store one day, and I saw her buy a can of Drāno. And I said to her, 'I didn't think you did that sort of stuff,'" in acknowledgment of Benoit Samuelson's well-known concern for the environment. Before the pair parted, Diane recalls, Benoit Samuelson "said to me, 'We need to go running some time' and I said to her, 'Joanie, your warm-up pace—is my race pace! Let's be REAL here!'"

Fortunately, Fournier and Robin Emery would come to appreciate one another's company and a rivalry. Robin said that she admired how Diane "was cool and calm before races, and I learned from her." Robin adds, "I remember running a sixteen-miler in Brunswick with Diane. We went stride for stride for eleven miles. I would probably have gone out too fast and died, but matching her pace made the race enjoyable."

Happy to support Dick Goodie's efforts to make some fairly young or outright inaugural road races welcoming to women as well as men, Diane became "First Woman" at several races in the early 1970s.

First, there was that previously mentioned Portland Elks Club thirteen-mile race (initially created in 1970 by Dick Goodie's Maine Masters Track Club and then known as the Elks Club race for the rest of its history) where Diane ran the course in 1 hour, 35 minutes, 30 seconds as the sole female. Robin captured the event in 1971, with Diane second. But then Diane ran off three straight victories, from 1972 to 1974, with Robin finishing second all three years. Diane ran her best time, of 1 hour, 26 minutes, 54 seconds in the 1972 event. Robin won the event back-to-back the last two years it was held, in 1978 and 1979. In 1978, Robin ran her best time on the course, 1 hour, 22 minutes, 26 seconds.

Started in 1964, the Lewiston Recreation Department 3-Mile Race had its first female entrant and sole woman in the field in 1972 when Diane Fournier participated and ran the course in 18:50. The author of this book, then a reporter with the *Lewiston Daily Sun*, was recently returned from completing Army basic training and advanced individual training at Fort Dix, New Jersey, just prior to joining the Maine Army National Guard, and entered the race as well. Finishing just behind Diane meant, for said author, several days of being teased for "being beaten by a girl!" at the newspaper office.

No women entered the race in 1973, but Diane returned to Lewiston in 1974, taking first place in a time of 17:01 and again beating schoolgirl Joan Benoit, who was second, with Karen Goodberlet third.

Diane says she remembers beating Joanie a total of three times (including this Lewiston race) in the early 1970s but "after that I only saw her backside!" Today, she'll occasionally tell the track athletes she coaches that "I beat her those couple of times—and half of them don't even know who she is!"

But the best memory for Diane at the 1974 Lewiston race actually involves a different Maine running legend, Ralph Thomas of Gardiner. The diminutive Penobscot Nation native racked up win after win around New England all through the 1970s, was a national-caliber Masters runner (forty years of age and older) and was inducted into the charter class of the Maine Running Hall of Fame when it was created in 1989. Ralph Thomas was known to start at the back of the field but then charge to the front in very short order (Ralph said he "liked to see the race develop" in front of him). In the 1974 race, Diane wasn't surprised to find Ralph back where she was at the outset. But, when he stayed right there, running alongside of her, as the field of runners began to space out, she became quite curious. "So, I said to him, 'Ralph, what are you doing HERE?' And he said, 'Oh, I just ran a marathon last week. I'm going to run with you.' That lasted . . . about three minutes . . . and he was gone!"

Diane was the first and only woman to participate in the 1972 Maine Masters Cape Elizabeth Turkey Trot, a 5.8-mile race first held in 1969. She was clocked in 38 minutes, 47 seconds.

In 1973 Diane was the first woman ever to participate in and complete the Androscoggin Lost Valley 9.2-mile race in Auburn, a race first begun in 1971. She ran the course in 66 minutes, 14 seconds.

And then there were a pair of races, a 5K and a 10K, held simultaneously at Portland's Riverside Industrial Parkway, sponsored, again, by the Maine Masters Track Club that began in 1970. Owing to the tragic death of Rollie Dyer, these races were renamed the Roland Dyer Memorial in 1972 and held until 1979. In 1972, Robin and Diane were the first two women to register and run the 10K, with Robin winning the race in 42 minutes, 48 seconds. And they were both present in 1973, with Robin winning in 41:27. Robin would win the 10K five straight years, lowering her time to a best of 37:26 in 1976, with Joan Benoit finishing second to her. In 1974 and again in 1975, Joan Benoit won the 5K race and then she won the 1979 10K race, in a time of 35:14, with Robin taking second place.

With all these races one trend becomes startling clear, when talking about Diane Fournier: she appears at Maine's road races less and less as the 1970s progressed.

Why? A very demanding teaching and coaching career. Fournier pursued a career in teaching physical education and was one of the original faculty at Mt. Ararat High School in Topsham.

"I started teaching in the fall of 1974 and coaching field hockey," Diane states, with no trace of resentment. Being on her feet all day, teaching and then coaching, she felt her legs getting tired in October and lasting that way throughout the school year. She didn't go to races in the fall and spring and only felt she had the time for them and felt rested enough during her off-time in the summer.

Diane taught and coached three sports, including field hockey, basketball, and track and field, for most of her forty-year career at Mt. Ararat; the 2016–2017 school year is her third year in retirement from teaching, but she still enjoys coaching.

Diane distinguished herself by becoming one of the most successful high school track and cross-country coaches in the state: her women's outdoor track teams won class A state championships in 1975 and 1992. Her indoor track team won state titles in 1993 and 1994, and her women's cross-country team of 1992 also won the state championship. Her teams also won many Kennebec Valley Athletic Conference titles in boys' and girls' cross-country and in girls outdoor track. She has also won two Central Maine Indoor League Championships in girls track.

Reflecting, today, on what it was like to run when most people didn't, especially females, Diane says, yes, there were moments she was uncomfortable or faced outright unpleasantness. Diane got used to receiving comments that reflected complete misunderstanding of what she was doing all the way up to verbal "abuse," training in her home area. "People would stop and say, 'Do you need a ride?' and I'd say, 'No, I'm just in a hurry!' But then there was stuff that was definitely more like mocking, so I learned to just ignore that." She remembers the specific instance when she and a friend were running a loop around a lake near her home—"and there was a big, fat guy, smoking a cigar, sitting on his deck and he'd say something to us every time we came by. So, one time I said to my companion, Norm, 'Want to do something with me?' And on their next loop, she stopped at the deck, took off her shoes, and offered them to him, saying, 'Here, Fat Man, here's a pair of shoes. Put them on—and try to keep up!' He never bothered us again. Norm said, "I don't believe you just did that. He's probably gonna kill us if he ever sees us on the road!""

As for unpleasant incidents during races, Diane only remembers two disturbing episodes, one in Maine and one in Connecticut.

Diane running the Casco Bay Marathon, 1980

In Maine, she says, there was one guy she beat regularly. He'd tried to outrun her—but she'd always beat him. And then he'd say to her, "I can't believe I'm letting a woman beat me." And I'd say, "What's wrong with that?" Diane recalls, "This guy so hated to be beaten by me and I'd always beat him. He'd race ahead. I'd maintain my pace—and I'd beat him, every time."

Another time she was running a four-mile race in Connecticut that was covered by a reporter representing a newspaper in New York. She had dueled with a male competitor for a better finishing place, a duel that found them going back and forth in front, then behind. "We were sprinting, and I beat him to the finish line. It was friendly. And when we got across the finish line, I turned around and we shook hands. Well, the reporter came to me asking all kinds of questions. Mostly he wanted to know: 'Do you always beat guys?' And I said, 'Well, yeah, those who are slower than me.' But when I saw the article, he put in all kinds of things I didn't say or didn't do; for the last line of it, he wrote that he saw the two of us, 'hand in hand, going off into the sunset to have dinner together.'"

That both Diane and Robin ran six-minute miles, well above average pace for men as well as women, is a testament to their abilities as runners. Diane thinks there are two important factors. "We spent more time outdoors than kids do today—and we were mentally tough." She recalls asking a well-regarded coach why he recruited runners so frequently from Maine: "He told me they don't race as much as everyone else and they train in tougher weather conditions."

Among her career highlights was her first race, the Boston Marathon in 1970. Also among her cherished memories was her best marathon, run in 2 hours, 58 minutes, 19 seconds at Casco Bay, in 1982, and a fifty-mile ultra-marathon in Brunswick, in 1981, when she clocked 7 hours, 23 minutes, 38 seconds. Over the years Fournier belonged to the Ararat Super Striders and the Central Maine Striders.

Fournier's other best times include: one mile, 5:29.9 (1981); two miles, 11:52.7 (1982); three miles, 17:52 (1981); 5K, 18:22; four miles, 24:16 (1982); five miles, 31:06 (1982); 10K, 38:14 (1982); ten miles, 66:24 (1983); 15K, 1:09:14 (1981); 13.1 miles, 1:26:22 (1982); fifteen miles, 1:40:44 (1982).

Once, Diane used to run with her student-athletes, but not anymore. "Even their jogging is faster than what I do," she says. Indeed, she doesn't race any more—and hasn't for quite some time.

"I'd rather run in the woods, with my dog. To be truthful, since I started with small groups, I really prefer those. I don't like big races," Diane says. The dog, a nine-year-old that is a reindeer herder by trade, requires regular exercising and represents one of her "three four-legged kids"; the other two are ferrets. "I can't run on the roads with my dog. She's the kind of dog that needs freedom, which is crazy. But I think running in the woods is the best thing for both of us."

But she still regularly attends races. "I've started to give back to road racing, by timing. I time the [Portland] Back Cove race every Wednesday once track season is over until they stop doing it, and I'll see people who will say, 'Oh, Diane, nice to see you. Remember when—' And I'll say,

'Oh yeah.' We've all gotten a bit older but they're still doing the road racing."

Diane is also part of a group that annually handles one of the water stops at the Portland marathon; to her chagrin, she sometimes sees girls running the marathon she could not get to run over 400 meters in high school—or could not get to run at all.

And is there anything she finds impressive about the running scene, today, in Maine? Diane says, "Just to see so many women running now. One of my former runners ended up fourth two years ago in the Portland marathon. At least they're running. I hear from a lot of my former students who say, 'because of you I'm running' and, of course, that means a great deal to me."

When she thinks back on the runners she shared the roads with, or just the runners she truly admires, Diane thinks immediately of Joan Benoit Samuelson; the "always respectful" talented runner and outstanding coach, Danny Paul of Falmouth High School; Kimberly Moody, professor of nursing at the University of Southern Maine, who won a number of marathons and ultra-marathon competitions; the late Andy Palmer of Madawaska, a "gentle giant" who posted one of the fastest marathons ever run by a Maine runner; and, of course—Robin.

Of the sport, she states, "There are so many things I've gotten out of running but probably the most is what it has done for me as an individual. I was a very introverted person once. I was an only child and very well protected growing up, and I've always done individual-type sports. It's certainly given me a lot of recognition among my peers, but the friends I've made through running—they are still there."

And, of her former rival, the woman with whom she shares the title of "First Woman to run the roads of Maine," Diane simply says of Robin Emery, "In just my second year of running I was grateful to find another half-crazy person who enjoyed running on the roads, running long and running fast. Unlike me, Robin had started running for herself while in college and she seemed to run for the simple fun of running, no other motivating factor. Since our first meeting we have enjoyed many races together as friends and competitors and have both observed the growth of women's running."

Diane runs ahead of Carlton Mendell in the fifty-mile ultra-marathon, Brunswick, 1980.

Diane adds, "Robin's awesome, the best. She's always upbeat. Always has a smile. We're good friends—though I haven't seen her in a while. If you didn't have a good day, she was there to help you out."

Diane Fournier concludes, "Yes, I remember Robin at a couple of races, because of the donut thing. Going to the starting line with it in her hand—and seeing the back side of her, after that—maybe it works, eating donuts."

FOUR

Portland Boys Club Race: "My God, There's a Broad! You Go Alice!"

THE BOSTON MARATHON, inaugurated in 1897, became the Boston Athletic Association's annual race to prepare its members to, essentially, become "more acquainted" with how to run—a marathon. The then-24.5-mile distance of the marathon had just been the featured event in the newly resurrected "modern" Olympics of 1896. Today, the Boston Marathon is recognized as the longest continuing, annual road race in the world.

And, quite frequently, the second-oldest annual road race in America is identified as the Portland (Maine) Boys Club 5-Mile Race. Both, traditionally, were run on Patriots' Day, the third Monday of April (earlier, for many, many years, the races were held on whichever day April 19 happened upon). In a very recent development, the race now called Portland Boys and Girls Club 5-Mile Race is now held on the Sunday before Patriots' Day Monday.

The connection between the two races seems obvious.

Patriots' Day, which honors the battles of Lexington and Concord, Massachusetts, on April 19, 1775, and the start of the American Revolutionary War, is celebrated in the United States *only* in the states of Massachusetts and Maine (the latter was part of Massachusetts until achieving statehood in 1820). So it should come as no surprise that Maine would eventually have a race of its own on a recognized day off for all schools and state offices.

Maine's oldest, continuing road race was launched in 1930. And right from its inaugural staging, the victor (Alvin Messer) ran a very creditable five-minute pace, and year after year the winning time would be in the twenty-six-minute or twenty-seven-minute range, with the occasional twenty-five-minute effort recorded, although, it is important to note that, until 1936, the course was actually closer to four and one-half miles (this was corrected in 1937). Over the first thirty-five years there were a few back-to-back or two-time winners, such as Russell Jellison (1931–1932), Herb DeVerber (1934–1935), Ed O'Connell (1953–1954), Paul Firlotte (1955–1956), Mike Kimball (1960, 1963) and some other celebrated Maine running legends would win, like Ed Shepard (in 1940, 1948) and the Mazzeo brothers (Dave, in 1941, and Bruno, in 1942).

The 1960s were dominated by Rockland's Bob Hillgrove, who won the race in 1962, ran off six straight wins, from 1964 to 1969, and then tacked on one more win in 1974, for a record total of eight victories in the historic race. The 1970s, stretching into the very early 1980s, found only one repeat champion, the charismatic, long-haired hometown boy, Ken Flanders, who captured seven total titles, including 1970, 1972, 1975, 1977, 1979, 1980, and 1981.

The most familiar name and face connected to the Portland Boys Club (PBC) race over its first fifty-plus years was easily its race director, the late Bart Peverada. He was proud to proclaim an association with the race dating right back to 1930, when he was photographed as one of the ten participants on the starting line for the inaugural event. When the Portland Boys Club Race turned fifty years old in April 1979, Peverada still had no blemishes on his record as having some connection with the historic race. Although Peverada did not finish the first event, he had either been a participant, a timer, or the race director for more than half a century.

In a 1983 piece about the history of the Boys Club race for the *Bangor Daily News*, Bob Haskell wrote of Peverada, "Yes, the race has a patriarch. His name is Bartholomew C. Peverada. The C stands for Caesar. He is 72. He was born and brought up in Maine's largest city and he was one of 10 runners to line up for the first race on Patriot's Day in 1930. They started from a crouch, as if they were going to run the 100-yard dash," Haskell added.

"I didn't finish," said the man everyone calls Bart and who entered the race three times. He finished the other two. "In 1935 I was supposed to be a timer," he told Haskell, "but my brother Tony and Andy Pettis, who was an employee at the Portland Boys Club, dared me to run. I finally said I would, but I was only going to go two blocks. Once we got going I felt pretty good and when I got down by the post office I got my second wind. It was the first time I had ever experienced a second wind. And, you know, I beat them both."

Peverada explained to Haskell that the race was actually run by the Boys Club's alumni association, of which he was president, and that a good share of the money the runners now paid to enter went toward the $1,000 in scholarships that the 175-member association gave to high school seniors every year. He also told Haskell that the race never had a fee until 1977 and "then we only made it a dollar. . . . The only thing the runners had to do before that was join the Maine AAU. Now the runners have to pay $3.00 before the day of the race and $4.00 on race day. I hope we don't have to go any higher."

While it is highly doubtful that anyone remembers, without having to look it up, Alvin Messer for his feat of winning the very first PBC race, the very controversial nature of just how women came to be part of the race, hopefully, ensures that Robin Emery and Diane Fournier will long be remembered and celebrated for their roles in its history.

Having already appeared and participated in Dyer-sponsored and Goodie-sponsored races in southern Maine in 1971, Robin and Diane were, of course, interested in the forty-plus-year-old race. It was a race, however, that required preregistration, although only thirty or forty men routinely appeared to run.

Dick Goodie determined that he must write a letter, making the case for the executive director of the Boys Club, Peverada, and his club officials to open the race to women and admit worthy, proven runners Robin Emery and Diane Fournier.

An austere man, given to wearing drab gray or black suits and a fedora hat, Peverada was almost never to be found with a smile on his face and looked like someone from central casting for a Hollywood drama from the 1930s. His stoic demeanor personified the strict standards he set for the race: the race must be conducted as it had *always* been conducted.

Haskell, in his 1983 piece, wrote of him, "As the man who has been associated with this race since the beginning, Bart Peverada has at times found himself bowing to the changing times. 'I would never let women in because I did not think they were strong enough to run five miles. I would never let in anyone under 16 because I did not think they were strong enough. I would never let in a high school kid unless I checked with his coach first.'" Women, of course, first joined the field in 1972. The race was opened to everyone, regardless of age, in 1977. That was also the first year that runners could register on the day of the race.

Portland newspaper sportswriter and columnist Vern Putney, who had worked at the Portland Boys Club before he secured his post with the newspaper, admired Peverada and loved the annual race. Putney would write, "in all the years I covered the race only once did Bart Peverada deliver bad news. He showed me two race applications, those of Robin Emery and Diane Fournier. The executive director had vetoed their entry."

Putney related, "I wouldn't settle for that! 'Go back to the club and tell them that females are the wave of the future!'—and that I don't wish a black eye for the Boys Club in the form of discrimination."

In his sweet, noncombative manner, Putney simply summed up the outcome this way: "Bart relayed the message, and I welcomed the lovely Robin at the starting line. Surely spring was in the air! She considered the early-morning takeoff from Ellsworth well worth the sacrifice."

It was actually quite admirable of Peverada to reverse course the very same year he was confronted with the controversy. On other issues he was not so willing to change course.

The author of this book, a member of the news staff for the *Portland Press Herald*, would write several guest columns about the race for the sports department during my tenure from 1972 to 1977.

Starting in 1973 I would run the race myself several years in a row and condemn Peverada's direction for:

- failing to provide any traffic control whatsoever, making a number of dangerous, four-way intersections with no traffic lights on the route a wait-where-you-are or make-it-across-if-you-can proposition for runners (one year I narrowly made it across Portland's infamous Marginal Way, ahead of an oncoming eighteen-wheeler);
- showing age discrimination, blocking entry to stellar teenage runner Robin Estey, who had just beaten me at an earlier 10K on the streets of Portland; and
- refusing to budge on his preregistration-only admission policy, creating the absurd situation where unregistered and numberless Hank Pfeifle would have won the race, but had to veer off the course a few yards short of the finish line and allow the second-best runner present on the day to "win" the event.

Haskell, in his 1983 article, wrote, "In 1976 . . . Hank Pfeifle, who had returned from Texas where he was going to school, was denied an official number on race day. But he ran anyway, Peverada recalled, and charged away from the rest of the field. Pfeifle turned left onto Chestnut, just before the finish line, and Cheverus High School's Jim Doane was declared the official winner. But Pfeifle had made his point. Post entries were accepted the next year. Pfeifle won the race in 1982, in a then-record time of 23:37.7."

Thanks to the efforts of Goodie and Putney, it was determined that the race, to be run in April of 1972, would allow women entrants, and Putney announced the fact a couple of weeks before in a *Portland Press Herald* story, carrying the headline "Maine Maidens May Gallop Way into PBC History." It identified Robin and Diane as being officially entered, and that both women happened to be twenty-five years old and teachers.

When the actual day arrived, and runners were milling about on Cumberland Avenue between the Portland Boys Club building and the Portland High School, the two women had very different reactions to another long-standing practice at the race: having to allow a physician to take their heart rates.

This practice probably owed to the same tradition in place at the Boston Marathon for many years. In one instance, the all-time men's champion (seven victories) at the race, the legendary Clarence DeMar, was given the test prior to the 1911 race, and was told that he had "heart murmurs," with the team of physicians advising him that he really should retire from distance running or, at the very least, should drop out "if he felt tired." DeMar wryly noted that he did not know if it were possible to run a marathon without feeling fatigue; nevertheless, he ran—and won—in a new course record, capturing the very first Boston title of his career. DeMar's last victory at Boston came in 1930, when he was nearly forty-two years old.

So Robin matter-of-factly joined the men in the line for the heart-rate test. When she presented herself before the physician, she started to pull her jersey up, as she had observed the men doing. Clearly embarrassed, the physician stopped her and said, "No! That won't be necessary," and that he could administer the test outside her clothing. Meanwhile, outside, incensed and viewing the procedure as completely "invasive," Diane refused to participate. Not surprisingly, the practice ended shortly thereafter.

While there was nothing unusual about Kenny Flanders racing off to victory, clearly, on the course, there was quite a bit of excitement that was brand-new. There were spectators who came to watch because they knew there were women in the race—and there were spectators who were to discover the fact only at the very fleeting moment it was happening.

The course runs down Cumberland to Forest Avenue, with a right-hand turn onto a cascading downhill, and subsequently a turn onto Baxter Boulevard, with the end of the first mile coming up shortly thereafter. The boulevard is a long, winding, and quite scenic tour, taking runners through a second- and third-mile route around the enclosed bay. Ultimately, runners are taken up onto the Washington Street bridge, wafting with the smells from the nearby baked bean factory, and then Washington Street itself, with pleasant smells emanating from a bread bakery and not-so-pleasant stale beer smells emanating from several outright dive bars. A turn onto Cumberland leads runners back through the Munjoy Hill section of Portland, crossing the aforementioned Marginal Way, and back to the start/finish line in front of the Portland Boys ("and Girls," as it known today) Club.

Robin and Dick Goodie, pacing together, 1972 Portland Boys Club Race

Robin was running with her friend, Dick Goodie, the talented Masters runner. A photograph of them together shows Robin, smiling, winging along seemingly without a care in the world. It was just another race. She was a few places ahead of Diane, and she was aware that, for a number of spectators, this wasn't business as usual; she could hear the words "girl" and "woman." One of her most lasting memories came, with a mix of bread and stale beer smells wafting into her nostrils, when she passed one of the bars on Washington Street. "We were hearing from the denizens of the bars along the street," and one of them suddenly shouted out, "My God, there's a broad! You go, Alice!" Diane would be treated to the shout, "There's *another* one!"

Clad in a bulky sweatshirt and sweatpants, Robin put in a strong fifth mile, speeding along the downhill section of Cumberland Avenue, eyes firmly upon the inverted "V" of spectators stretching out before her, enveloping the finish line. A wonderful finish line portrait shows her smiling, looking hardly taxed at all by her effort.

Dick Goodie playfully wrote to her, of that finish-line picture, "After the blistering pace you set the fifth mile, the picture shows you hardly breathing. You really know how to hurt a guy. That's me thrashing home a half-mile over your left shoulder."

And Vern Putney, in a personal note he sent to her, along with his Portland newspaper race coverage clippings, said, "You added a lot of charm as well as life in your first-gal home in the Boys Club race. . . . Golly, you'll be tough to catch in the glamor department. Think your time will be tough to beat. Again, so nice of you to make history."

Robin Emery, wearing a hand-printed Number "22," was the forty-fourth finisher and Diane Fournier placed fifty-second at the forty-third annual Portland Boys Club Race, in 1972, as the first two women ever to run and finish the race. Robin ran the course in 33 minutes, 03 seconds. Diane completed the course in 34 minutes, 55 seconds. And coming in as the very last two participants to complete the course, in sixty-ninth and seventieth place, in the same time of 43 minutes, 18 seconds, Mr. and Mrs. Thomas Dodge ran the race together, with Sheila Dodge becoming the third woman in that historic race.

The headline for the *Portland Press Herald*'s account of the race read, in big, bold lettering: "Flanders Sets Record" with a secondary heading above it, "71 (3 Gals) in Boys Club Race." The newspaper's sports editor, Roland Wirths, began his account: "Ken Flanders, a dominant figure in Maine distance running circles, won the first co-educational Portland Boys Club five-mile race with shocking ease Monday, setting a record in the process." Wirths noted that the race had attracted a record field of entrants, with seventy-one starters, with all but one finishing.

Leading from the start, a trademark move of his, Flanders ran 24 minutes, 48 seconds, which broke the record established by Bob Hillgrove in 1969, when the Rockland star ran the course in 25 minutes, 03 seconds.

Ken Flanders remembers, "I was a freshman at Northeastern University, in Boston, starting in the fall of 1971. In the spring of 1972, I had never run a road race in the Boston area at that time although I had done several in Maine. I had never competed in an event with women.

Further, Northeastern didn't have women's cross-country or track, and I don't think any college in America did. My college coaches gave me permission to run the 1972 PBC road race. It was the first year women competed. I remember being inside the Boys Club building—where I wasn't worried about losing to one of them!

"We picked up our numbers and pinned them to our chests. We went through a heart monitor line with a doctor, and I wondered if they took the female runners to another location.

"Yes, I won that day, and I do hope I congratulated all three female runners who were there after the event (I honestly don't remember). And, yes, I do remember that a woman named Robin was the first to finish the race. . . . Frankly, it took me a while to take women's running seriously. But I did."

Both Robin and Diane were "announced" as entered for the forty-fourth PBC Race on Patriots' Day, 1973, but on race day Robin and Brook Morrow were the only two women to participate. And the Portland Boys Club officials were ready—with trophies for the first and second females at the race.

Portland Press Herald sports editor Wirths wrote that race account too, identifying Robin as "attractive," and quoting her as being "satisfied" with her winning time of 32:24, having shaved almost forty seconds off her time from the year before, and posting an overall finishing place of thirty-third. Morrow finished in a time of 42:54.

Wirths continued his profile of Robin, noting that the low-handicap golfer and fifth-grade teacher had started as a jogger in college. "I didn't run seriously until the last two years," she explained and then responded this way when Wirths asked her how the men in the race regarded her: "The men don't seem to mind having me run with them. In fact, they're pretty nice about it."

Doing a follow-up column on the race, Vern Putney answered some lingering questions about perennial race favorite Ken Flanders's "disappearance" and the victory in the race by Steve Jaynes. He also loved to include notes about those "back in the pack." This was the first appearance in the race for this book's author and Putney, who loved employing all kinds of word-play involving discussions of females (he was frequently

Robin crosses the finish line of the 1972 Portland Boys Club Race, the first woman ever to do so, in this news clipping photograph from the pages of the Portland Press Herald.

given to using the phrase "distaff side") and female pulchritude quoted me for his piece.

Identifying me as "the cityside newsman" and 1971 Northeastern University graduate, Putney wrote that I "found the scenery a great nature walk" and then quoted me as saying, "'Even back as far as I was,' joked bird-lover Rice, 'I appreciated the view of Robin.'"

In my first guest column for the *Maine Sunday Telegram* sports section, I wrote a personal account of my experience. The headline-writer had some fun, titling it "Tattered by Time and Distance, a Runner's Job Gets Lonelier," and then, in an homage to the popular film *Love Story*, he added a "kicker" (secondary headline, in smaller letters just above the principal title) that read "Is 47th Place Having to Say You're Sorry?" I, of course, did not know Robin at the time.

Concerning Robin, I wrote, "I ran with one group, then another, and another. It was interesting watching them all move on. As I ultimately reached Baxter Boulevard I was passed first by a beautiful young woman and then by a youth who I must be at least one foot taller than. They came—and passed me—in all shapes and sizes."

The piece closed with my failed attempt to overtake a runner a few hundred yards from the finish, only to be surprised when he suddenly veered off the course, still ahead of me but not crossing the finish line.

I crossed the finish line then chased him down to find out why he hadn't completed the race, only to discover he hadn't registered to run officially and was told specifically NOT to cross the finish line. I closed my column with, "It figures . . . beaten even by a 'noncontestant.'"

I used to "joke" that I was using the annual Portland race to "get into shape for softball season." It was the only race I'd enter all year long, and, for the record, I ran 35 minutes, 09 seconds, or a seven-minute-per-mile pace. Robin, of course, was running six-minute-and-less-than-30-seconds, per-mile pace.

In 1974, Robin won her third straight PBC race, finishing in thirty-seventh place, and once again, significantly improving her time, clocking 31:08. Diane was the forty-ninth finisher overall and a Cape Elizabeth High School student named Joan Benoit debuted at the race, finishing in 34:51 and sixty-seventh place overall *[I would like "the world" to take note of the fact that I, Ed Rice, "beat" Joanie that day, running 34 minutes, 20 seconds, for fifty-eighth place overall!].*

Robin won her fourth straight Portland, in 1975, again lowering her time, to 29:10; this time was almost two minutes faster than her time from her record-setting third-year victory.

"Amazingly," wrote Putney, "33 of the record 99 starters were under the swift half-hour pace. Joan Benoit, Cape Elizabeth High School smooth strider who may one day challenge [Robin], missed that coveted time mark by five seconds."

A record of thirteen women were entered. Robin's four-in-row victories read: 33:03, 32:24, 31:08 and 29:10—and, of course, she had a specific goal in 1975 to try to break the thirty-minute barrier for five miles.

Portland Press Herald sports reporter Augie Favazza wrote the 1975 PBC account, noting that Robin was the first female finisher, taking twenty-sixth place in a time of 29:10. He described her at the finish line this way: "Did I break the 30-minute mark," she asked of anyone who looked like an official. "Maybe I wound up in the top 20," she added when a bystander told her she did crack the thirty-minute mark in bettering her old record of 31:08 for best time by a woman. Joan Benoit was the next top female, with 30:05 clocking in thirty-fourth place. "Joan was with me for three miles, but her best is shorter ones," Robin added, proving not to be anywhere near as good a prophet as she was a runner!

At the 1976 Portland Boys Club Race, Joan Benoit broke Robin's four-straight victory streak, with a win in a new course record of 28:19, breaking Robin's course record (29:10) by fifty-three seconds and finishing twentieth overall. Robin, dealing with a blister, hobbled home in fort-first place in 30:56. What bothered her, slightly, after the race was having to accommodate the Portland newspapers photographer, who insisted she wait around and then accompany him, to go into another area, and allow him to photograph both of the racing champions together, with Joan, and feeling like she had to "smile" while Joan held the champion's trophy.

In the Favazza article, Joan, who was representing the Liberty AC, "credits Robin, whom she terms Maine's women's distance pioneer, with encouraging her, and many others, to take up interest in the longer events."

In another Vern Putney follow-up piece, after the race, Joan was credited with not only having the fastest time for a woman but the highest finish, twentieth place, ever posted by a woman. Joanie was then an eighteen-year-old and said, by Putney, to be in her "first year-round campaign"; she was also quoted as saying it was her first time beating Robin in "about eight tries."

In a 2015 article for the *Ellsworth American*, Taylor Vortherms noted that "it would take the first-ever women's Olympic marathon gold medalist to end Emery's long time winning streak in Maine" and quoted the then-fifty-seven-year-old Joan Benoit Samuelson as saying, "Robin had a huge impact on me. She was beating me. Then, she sort of passed the baton to me. . . . Robin was a real pioneer. She was running well before women were accepted in the sport."

The 1976 race was also significant because the "real" winner of the race was not allowed to win; this was the year of the infamous incident involving Hank Pfeifle.

Pfeifle remembers, "I had just moved back from Texas where I had run well for two years. I was eager to mix it up in Portland again after having had a taste of this great race in 1974 while living in Rangeley. The Boys Club race was a very established race with great history and prestige. There were only a handful of races in New England that had such a long and distinguished history. As you know (but I didn't) the PBC race was preregistration only—no exceptions. 'Ah,' I attempted to argue, 'but I came all the way over from New Hampshire.' Response: 'Sorry, kid, but we'll cut you some slack. You can race but don't go across the finish line.' I thought to myself: 'Um, well, okay.' So that's what I did and I must confess to being more determined than ever to win. People were shocked when I ducked into the crowd ten yards from the finish. I felt a bit like the kid in the film *Loneliness of the Long Distance Runner*, but I had to live up to my end of the bargain. It is satisfying to know that the next year the registration rules were relaxed to allow 'day of' participation. Officially winning in 1983 with a course record at the time was especially satisfying. I loved that race."

The 1977 race found world-class distance runner Lynn Jennings, from nearby Newmarket, New Hampshire, capturing the race and missing matching Benoit's course record by just one second, in 28:20. Benoit was second, and Robin third.

Robin would miss the 1978 and 1979 Portland Boys Club races when she ran back-to-back Boston Marathons on Patriots' Day.

In a prepublicity piece for the 1980 PBC in the Portland newspapers, Robin was welcomed back to the race and listed as a favorite. She noted, "I love this course. It's so flat, I could fly." She won in 29:41, with second- and third-place women posing no real threat. She was about to start a new streak at the storied race.

She won her second straight and sixth overall title in 1981, beating a New Hampshire woman by over two minutes. Her time of 29:06 beat her best previous time at the race by four seconds. The men's title was captured, again, by Ken Flanders.

"Maybe they should call it the Kenny and Robin show," wrote Allen Lessels in the *Portland Press Herald*. There "wasn't a woman near her," he wrote, and Robin told him, "I was flying today. I looked around at the

Kenny Flanders, Robin, and Danny Paul at the 1975 Portland Boys Club race

start and didn't see anyone who looked real fast. I passed two women in front of the Boys Club (just a couple hundred yards into the race) and didn't see any others."

Asked by Lessels to explain her success at PBC, Robin replied, "I can't believe it," adding simply, "I really do well on a flat course like this. I hate hills and where we live it's all mountains. There is always one hill to spoil your time."

She said she didn't mind the 180-mile drive from Lamoine. "This is a big win for me, since it's on somebody else's home turf. And this was my best [time] here ever."

The 1982 race was more of the same. She won her seventh women's title, in 29:39, finishing sixty-eighth out of 273. The second-place woman was over two minutes behind her as she captured her third-straight PBC title.

Jerry Crasnick of the *Portland Press Herald* wrote, "Ten years ago, Robin Emery struck a blow for women runners by entering the race. . . . Since then, she has become as much of an institution as the race itself. The 35-year-old Emery maintained her perennial position as top female finisher. While she cracks more senior citizen jokes than George Burns, she shows no signs of slowing down."

"Every year I expect some little kid to come whizzing by me. Winning feels great. I'm still waiting for old age to catch up with me. It hasn't yet," she told Crasnick, who noted of Robin that she "looks more like 18 than 35."

"I just wanted to break 30 minutes and come in first," Robin told him. "Every mile was six minutes or below. I don't even look around at the competition anymore. Today I just went out there and trucked."

Crasnick closed his piece noting that "Flanders will be back" (he lost to Hank Pfeifle). . . . And so will a 35-year-old institution named Robin Emery." Robin was clearly feeling the pressure before the 1983 race. She told Crasnick in a prerace article, "'Every year it's a big deal,' says Emery. 'People say, "Will the old lady be able to do it again?" I can't even have fun anymore. But I'll be there, unless I get in a car wreck along the way.'"

Crasnick commented, "Emery . . . talks as if her body is ready for the salvage heap. But history shows that while she's getting older, she's getting better, too." He noted that in the last year she had won her seventh title, despite a back injury that put a crimp in her training. For that year's race, she told Crasnick that she was in peak shape, having run sixty-five miles per week, and lifting weights every other day all winter. She also told him that "the Boys Club course was her favorite."

Crasnick's race account for 1983 flatly stated that Robin "cruised home" for her eighth PBC victory and "made it look easy," winning her fourth straight title while finishing seventy-third overall. Her time of 29:19 was only thirteen seconds off her best time ever posted. Still, he noted, it was "well ahead" of the 29-minute, 39-second effort she turned in the previous year.

Emery, the writer stated, was "typically upbeat" after the race. "I didn't see any other women. But I wasn't looking for them. When we hit the wind on the bridge I was just looking for some big men to run behind. I couldn't find any of them either," she quipped. The second woman finished in 31:32.

Crasnick then wrote a second account, for the afternoon *Portland Evening Express*. It was published under the title "Emery Wins 8th PBC Women's Crown." His opening sentences read, "Ms. Emery simply doesn't do her justice anymore. From here on in, we might as well refer to her as the First Robin of Spring. She is Robin Emery, and for the past 11 years she has made a habit of finishing first among women in the Portland Boys Club road race. Since crashing the party on Patriots' Day in 1972, Emery has won eight PBC women's titles—including two strings of four straight."

After mentioning that the "first string" of four straight came from 1972 to 1975, he noted that "Yesterday the 36-year-old Lamoine schoolteacher notched the second, defeating Bethany Heslam by better than two minutes in the 54th annual PBC five-mile race."

He continued, "While 'Emery wins again' makes for a boring headline in comparison, Robin herself was as jubilant over No. 8 as No. 1."

She stated, "This race has always meant a lot to me. Up where I live runners don't get all this attention and the TV cameras. I've been edgy all day about it. I didn't have to drive down until 7:30 this morning, and I still got up at 4:00."

However, Crasnick noted, "Emery showed no signs of nervousness once the race began." Her winning time of 29:19 was thirteen seconds off her PBC best, and "worlds better" than her 33-minute, 04-second time in 1972, the writer stated. The "only obstacle was a brutal headwind" on Tukey's Bridge, but by then, Cranick wrote, "Emery was too far ahead for it to matter."

There was something special to Robin related to the 1983 race, and both journalists who covered the event picked up on it in their coverage.

Emery dedicated her victory to her father Gordon, who died in December of 1982. "My Dad loved coming to watch me run," she told Crasnick. "He would always come to this race and take pictures along the way. I decided to try and win it for him. When my legs started hurting at the end, thinking of him kept me going."

Bob Haskell of the *Bangor Daily News* covered race as well, noting rather memorably for Robin in his opening sentence that "Two men from northern Maine and a schoolmarm from Hancock County captivated southern Maine with their remarkable running talents." Haskell noted that Robin had won for the fourth straight time and for the eighth time in twelve years. Her time was exactly, he stated, one minute off Benoit's course record, set in 1976.

"The wind was just like a hand pushing against you," she told Haskell. "I was running all by myself when it hit me. There weren't any men to hide behind." She was "more than satisfied with her performance," she explained, noting that she "has dedicated this year to her late father, who died in December. It was her third victory in as many starts."

In 1984, Robin was looking for a fifth straight Portland Boys Club title when she was beaten by a schoolgirl, Leslie Walls of Biddeford. Even at the hands of defeat in the 1984 event, Emery said moments after the race, "Oh well, it happens to all of us." After acknowledging her superb record at the Bangor Labor Day Race, Lessels noted, "The story is only slightly different at the Portland Boys Club race where the competition is among the keenest in the state. Since first winning in '72, Emery has lost just twice *[Author's note: It was really three times, Lynn Jennings, 1977]*— this year to a talented 17-year-old Biddeford runner, Leslie Walls, and in '76 when Joan Benoit whizzed through the course in 28:19 record time."

And in 1985, she was second again, "this time to a ringer, Lynn Jennings, who has been racing back at her world-class level in recent months."

In 1986, she told Portland writer Allen Lessels she hadn't minded coming in second last year to Jennings in 1985, stating simply—"she's a star." But the year before, 1984, had been less palatable. "It was pouring that day. My shoe came untied. It was just a bad race. I was really mad about that. If you lose when you're doing your best, it's okay. But if you're doing something wrong—"

In the 1986 PBC race Emery passed Wanda Haney about halfway through and moved out to a thirty-second win. Her 29:17 time was two seconds better than her winning time in 1983. She'd won the 1981 race in her all-time best of 29:06. Haney was a 1985 graduate of South Portland High School, who won cross-country, 880, and mile titles as a senior. She was then running for St Joseph's College, training with coach Brian "Ziggy" Gillespie.

When Robin Emery won in 1986, it was for the ninth time in the fifteen years women had been allowed to compete. Lessels started the piece, "Robin Emery is back—back with a new name [Rappa, having married educator Joseph Rappa in 1985] new training methods, and renewed determination."

Wrote Lessels, "A 30-ish-looking woman who calls herself, 'the old lady of road racing,' Emery nevertheless has the spirit of a young filly and, like a girl, she giggles. And she has managed to retain her sense of humor and perspective."

What about the pressure of winning? "I woke up at 4:30 this morning, scared," Emery said of the PBC race. "I hate it. The pressure is hard to take because everybody expects too much."

The day before, the *Maine Sunday Telegram*, as usual, had predicted her victory.

The year 1986 would prove to be Robin Emery's last victory at Maine's oldest road race. With her marriage, she would move to Massachusetts and not return to live in the state of Maine year-round until 2000.

And almost one-quarter of a century since she'd won the very first Portland Boys Club race attended by women, Robin did attempt to slip quietly into the 1996 race. She believes her friend Dick Goodie tipped off

Winning the Portland Boys Club race in 1974 or '75—Robin is not sure which victory it was!

the greater Portland media that she was in attendance, and she wound up doing a number of interviews, running the course uneventfully.

Today, Robin Emery says she'd like "to run the Portland Boys Club race just one more time," perhaps just to "hear the echoes" one more time and celebrate a legacy at the race no runner—man or woman—is ever likely to equal or surpass.

FIVE

Bangor Labor Day 5-Mile Race: "Okay [to Run], My Dear—But Just Don't Get in the Way"

IF THE HISTORY OF RUNNING ROAD RACES in the state of Maine matters to people, say fifty or even one hundred years or more from now, one can only wonder how impressed those individuals will have to be with the legacy of one Robin Emery at Maine's second-oldest road race, the Bangor Labor Day 5-Mile Race. She won the race fourteen of the first seventeen years she attended it, from 1972 to 1988, and she captured a fifteenth and final title, in 1998, when she was just one month shy of her fifty-second birthday.

The Bangor Labor Day race was first conducted in 1963, when eight men lined up on Main Street, Bangor, in front of the Paul Bunyan statue, and set off. The original, challenging route, used for several decades, was actually closer to 5.2 miles, with "5.17" as the figure most frequently used. The course would not be properly measured for 5.0 miles (tinkering with the finish by eliminating the trek around the horse track) and certified as such until 1985.

The original route—most of which remains intact today—travels down West Main Street, paralleling and within view of the Penobscot River, and heads toward downtown Bangor for a fast first mile. It makes a sharp left-hand turn onto Exchange Street and then requires runners to negotiate a dangerous (if left unpatrolled, which it was for much of the race's early history) four-way intersection at Exchange and State streets, proceeding straight through Exchange, past City Hall and onto Harlow Street, passing the Bangor Public Library and the old Bangor High School. This equally fast second mile leads runners down to a meandering stretch of Kenduskeag Avenue, aptly named as it parallels the Kenduskeag Stream on the runners' right.

Entering the third mile, the runner who has raced just a little too fast than he or she should have prudently done is about to pay a steep price—literally and figuratively. A sharp left turn off pavement leads to the infamous "14th Street Extension," a short stretch of severe incline, on a path through the woods, leading back onto pavement, and the continuing uphill climb, on Holland Street, a lesser-known side street of Bangor's West Side. The climb doesn't end until runners emerge facing a main thoroughfare, Ohio Street, which must be crossed at the runner's own risk. A short, flat stretch, on Wiley Street, leads to another main thoroughfare, Union Street, which, again, must be crossed at the runner's own risk. On Union Street, runners face another daunting, short but steep uphill climb, to be completed just before making a sharp right-hand turn onto West Broadway. Historic West Broadway is one of Bangor's stately old original streets, wide for horse-and-carriage vehicles and featuring some of the lavish old captains' and lumbering barons' mansions from Bangor's nineteenth-century fame as the "lumbering capital of the world." The sight of the occasional granite horse-hitching post adds to the charm.

For the runner who has wisely conserved energy, the race's fourth mile offers a speedy flat or slightly downhill stretch—unless the nasty convergence of West Broadway intersecting with a major thoroughfare, Hammond Street, has forced a dead stop in the instance of a runner's unfortunate timing of arriving at the same point where a vehicle has the right of way. Continuing farther down West Broadway, runners make a left onto Buck Street, and another long, gently downhill stretch, passing the Bass Park racetrack complex and old Bangor Auditorium on their right.

Now, for the old, original course, the runner was well into the fifth mile of the race; runners made a sharp right turn at the end of Buck and back onto Main Street, retracing their steps past the Paul Bunyan statue.

Not only were runners not done upon reaching the statue, but the next diabolical stretch seemed almost unfair. First, there was a long uphill, leading into the parking area for the Bangor Auditorium and the race-track complex. Then runners were required to race right onto the heavy-sand surface (which turned into outright muck on a rainy day) of that race track, replete with horse droppings to slalom past, and a near-complete circling of the track was required, with the finish line coming right in front of the grandstands.

It was no wonder you rarely saw a runner complete the old course, with a smile or looking anything but greatly fatigued.

Dave Farley, a great Brewer High School and Brown University runner, who made a national name for himself as a miler during a period when that distance was the glamor running event in the country (even appearing in competitions with the legendary Jim Ryun), won the Labor Day race in its first two years, clocking 26 minutes, 55 seconds in 1963 and 28:40 in 1964. Given the difficulty of the third and fifth miles and the fact that the course was two-tenths longer than five miles, it really is no surprise that the times are frequently high even for the quality of runner being talked about.

From 1965 to 1969, the race's all-time male champion (with seven total victories) Bob Hillgrove of Rockland, frequently dubbed "Maine's King of the Roads" in this era, reeled off five straight wins. Twice he lowered the existing record, with a best of 26 minutes, 44 seconds in 1968. In back-to-back record-breaking performances Walt Renaud won in a time of 25:58, and arguably the most legendary male Masters runner of this era, Ralph Thomas, captured the first of two titles in Bangor, with an excellent time of 25:43.

Once the so-called running boom of the mid-1970s was unleashed the race quite often was—and continues to this day to be—a front-page story for the *Bangor Daily News*, with writers seeking both principal and secondary aspects of the race to present and multiple runners always interviewed for their perspectives.

Back in 1972, the race made for just the briefest of accounts, often written by someone who knew little about running and could not have cared less about it. Indeed, the account was frequently presented without the writer's name, or "byline," in journalism parlance—as was the case for the unnamed 1972 account.

For the men, it really deserved to have been given a top billing, based on all the "Top Guns" present for the occasion. There was Hillgrove—and Thomas—and, from southern Maine, two of the state's most notable schoolboys, Ken Flanders from Portland and Larry Greer from Cape Elizabeth. In what wound up being a very tactical race, with a lead pack of six worthy rivals punching and counter-punching, Greer emerged victorious, in a time of 26 minutes, 33 seconds.

But unlike all the sound and fury that had attended the entry and presence of Robin Emery and Diane Fournier in Portland, for that spring's Portland Boys Club race, there was absolutely no prerace concerns or publicity because the Bangor race allowed race-day registering.

Robin remembers: "So, I walked into the old auditorium where they were registering runners and I said to them [race officials handling registrations], 'Do you mind if I run?'—And they kind of looked—and seemed to be thinking to themselves, 'Should we do this and let her in?' and they got together and talked it over, and, finally, one of them said to me, almost in a whisper: 'Okay, my dear, but just don't get in the way.'"

A total of forty-six runners started the race, with two males dropping out; only one participant was female. Being the *only* female present, with absolutely no media fuss, meant Robin had absolutely no reason to be nervous. She says, matter-of-factly, "so I ran—and I didn't die." She notes, "Yes, they gave me a number, but there was shocked silence when I came through the finish."

And, equally matter-of-factly, the *Bangor Daily News* reported, in the third paragraph of its following day's account, "The race was unique in one respect, Robin [Emery] of Ellsworth finished 24th in 33 minutes, 21 seconds and was the first woman competitor in the race's history."

Fortunately, there turns out to be a very qualified, very respectful eyewitness to this history, a noted Maine runner, race creator, and race official, who says, "My first encounter with Robin was at the tenth Bangor Labor Day 5-Mile Road Race on a warm Monday, September 6, 1972."

Later to be cofounder of the Down East Striders club, based in Bangor, and cocreator of such wonderful events as the Benjamin's 10K and the

Cranberry Island 5K (and a 2016 inductee of the Maine Running Hall of Fame), Larry Allen was a seventeen-year-old member of the Mount Desert Island High School cross-country team, brought that very year to Bangor for the race.

He remembers his coach, Howie Richard Jr., had taken a vanload of the runners from the team to Bangor "for perhaps a bonding exercise or a maybe just a little toughening up." It was Larry Allen's first road race.

Allen recalls that the race was happening midway through the Munich Olympics, just five weeks after the US track team, featuring such stars as Steve Prefontaine, Frank Shorter, Dave Wottle, Jim Ryun, Jeff Galloway, Jack Bacheler, Kenny Moore, and Coach Bill Bowerman, had actually spent ten days training in Maine, at Bowdoin College, before departing for Germany.

Further, Allen notes, "It was a frightening time." There was no end yet in sight for the Vietnam War. The tragic attack on the Israeli athletes at the Olympics had happened in the twenty-four hours just prior to that Labor Day race, and there was an unanswered question of whether the Olympics could or should be resumed. The Watergate break-in had happened just a couple of months previously and the reelection of Richard Nixon was looming two months ahead.

The professional artist that Larry Allen is provides us with this wonderful portrait: "We were a pack of about forty runners lined up on Main Street beneath the Paul Bunyan statue for that midday start. Among the runners were eight or nine future Maine Running Hall of Fame members. There was a palpable hubbub among spectators, race officials, and runners alike because among us was the first woman to sign up to run the event in its history. Robin was twenty-five. She was tall, striking, fearless, and full of good cheer. She possessed a certain grace in her very presence."

He continues, "I'm not sure I had ever even seen a woman runner in person at that point in my life. I remember everyone in the field of participants being accepting and respectful of a woman in the race and doing our best to treat her as 'one of the boys'; some were a tad concerned about being beaten by 'a girl' but more in a self-deprecating way, perhaps mocking their own lack of preparation for the run than anything."

And the race itself?

"When the race started, I just wanted to cover the distance," Allen states. "It was twice as far as I had ever run in a race and doing so on paved city streets was an altogether new experience. I fell in with a few of my teammates and Howie. Robin was just ahead of us. It was impossible not to notice the grace and ease of her long loping strides."

He adds, "Spectators through downtown Bangor did a double-take when they'd see her coming along. They'd smile and inevitably respond by cheering or saying 'Look, a woman!' or 'Wow, look at her go!' She eventually pulled away from us on the wide, elegant downhill section of West Broadway, near the eventual home of Stephen King. It was clear to even those concerned about being beaten by a woman that her strength, competitiveness, and grace wasn't something to be a chauvinist about; instead, she was someone to be admired and respected."

Of his longtime friend, Robin, Larry Allen now concludes: "At age twenty-five, it was Robin's first of fifteen victories in the landmark event. Her last win came twenty-seven years later, at age fifty-one. I remember hearing that race organizers hadn't even made an accommodation for a woman's trophy for her first victory. In a perfect turn, the trophy for the woman's winner is now named in her honor."

When Robin returned for the 1973 race, she was, again, the sole women in a forty-nine-member field to start the race on a brutally hot (eighty-four degrees) and muggy day; that race started shortly after 2:00 p.m., a starting time that had evolved into something of a tradition for the race. Of the forty-three individuals who crossed the finish line, Robin was thirty-first in a time of 34 minutes, 46 seconds. And, for the occasion, the race organizers had a trophy for her—albeit one that featured a figure of a male basketball player! As she told Taylor Vortherms, for a feature story for the *Ellsworth American* in April of 2015, "I wasn't going away. So they figured they'd give me something for showing up." The *Bangor Daily News* account, for its Tuesday morning paper in September of 1973, was written by Bob Haskell, who provided eyewitness details in telling the story of a second straight win by Larry Greer.

Many years later, Bob Haskell, former reporter and sports editor for the *Bangor Daily News* (and Keith L. Ware Award winner, the Department of the Army's top journalism prize for military journalists) says,

"Before Joan Benoit captured our hearts, Robin Emery caught our attention. At least that's how it worked for me. Robin was one of the first women athletes—perhaps the very first—with whom I dealt on a regular basis after joining the *Bangor Daily News'* sports staff in 1973. Robin is one of my examples of how many events, especially sports events, that we define as news follow an annual cycle and how we associate specific people with those specific events. Consequently, we identify certain people, such as Robin Emery, with certain annual events, such as Bangor's five-mile Labor Day road race."

Bob further reflects, "Robin Emery became a personality in the annual Bangor race, but her star usually rose and shined bright for one day at a time because of the timing of the event," explaining that the first Monday in September generally marked the end of the summer season for his five-man Sports Desk, which was frequently understaffed, right then, because of vacations. "It was a day to catch our breath, most years, because everyone was back at work and before we all plunged into the high school and college fall sports season the very next day."

But right from the very beginning the race and distance running itself mattered to Bob Haskell, and it showed in his detailed coverage.

Haskell remembers, "It was fun to cover the road race because it was run during the day—mostly in the early afternoon and then in the morning, as I recall—and there was this luxury of being able to talk to some of the runners and then have plenty of time to write the story before the 8:30 p.m. all-edition deadline. That's how Robin got her fifteen minutes of fame for one day a year before quickly being forgotten during the crunch of soccer matches, field hockey contests, cross-country meets, and football games that followed."

The award-winning journalist continues, "I don't recall Robin making a very big deal about doing something special on behalf of women—even though the idea of women running FIVE WHOLE MILES was not universally understood in the mid-1970s. She did not see herself as a feminist pioneer for the running boom which gripped the baby boomers a few years later because no one knew that boom was coming. She was Robin. She loved to run. Period."

Haskell also enjoyed that Robin was always pleasant and could even be feisty with him, and she had a good memory: "Robin was always a pleasure to chat with for a few minutes before the Bangor race and then interview after she had finished—as either the only woman or the first woman—after we came to identify one another as belonging in that place on that day. I referred to her as the 'schoolmarm from Ellsworth' one year when I wrote of her running in yet another Labor Day race in Bangor. 'Hey, Haskell. What's the idea of calling me *a schoolmarm?*' she asked me when she ran in Bangor the next year."

In 1974, Robin arrived to discover, for the first time in three years, there was to be a second woman in the race. Robin set a new women's course record of 31 minutes, 41 seconds, taking twenty-fourth place overall, with the talented eighteen-year-old Joan Westphal finishing in thirty-first place, in 33:34.

And in 1975, Robin won her fourth consecutive Bangor race, in 32 minutes, 26 seconds, as the twenty-seventh finisher overall. It was Joan Westphal in second place again, 57 seconds behind, in 33:23, and a thirty-second place finish overall. Two other females ran and completed the course, in what was a record field of fifty-seven starters.

Robin would miss the 1976 race, and Westphal would capture the women's division. But Robin returned to the race in 1977 with a vengeance, setting yet another new course record for women, clocking 30 minutes, 42 seconds. On the men's side, the legendary Bob Hillgrove, too, returned to Bangor to win his seventh and final title, still making him the men's all-time champion for total wins. He did it in style, all-time men's champion Bob Hillgrove beating Ralph Thomas's existing course record of 25:43, set in 1971, by nineteen seconds, with a splendid 25:24 effort.

Today, Bob Hillgrove recalls enjoying sharing the spotlight with Robin, as respective men's and women's champions, at both the Portland Boys Club race and the Bangor Labor Day race: "But, for me, the BEST moment we had together, was the '77 Labor Day 5-Miler where we BOTH set records. I have these color photos of us, side by side, in a sealed scrapbook, plus I have some super 8-millimeter film of the event that runs eleven minutes. These are very special to me."

Bob Hillgrove, the all-time men's champion with seven victories, crosses the finish line first on the Bass Park horse track of the original Bangor Labor Day race course.

Hillgrove would return to the Bangor race more than twenty years later in 1998, to run and be recognized for his extraordinary history of excellence, with the presentation of "a retired number" at the awards ceremony. And, at that very race, coming up one month shy of her fifty-second birthday, he would witness Robin Emery capturing her fifteenth victory. "I got to give her a BIG HUG after she won," he noted.

Finally, Hillgrove remarks, "Anything that can be said, that can be written about the greatness of Robin Emery is well DESERVED. It's been a great ride."

In 1978, Robin won for the second straight time (and her sixth victory in the 1970s) and lowered her course record, for the third time in the decade, with a time of 30 minutes, 31 seconds. A couple of months before the 1979 race Robin was involved in another summer bicycle accident that made racing "all out" difficult for her by the time Labor Day rolled around and explains fairly easily why another woman could beat her with time of over 34 minutes. When Jamie Dunn won the race, in 1979, Robin took third place, her one and only "loss" for the entire decade.

In 1980, *Bangor Daily News* columnist Bob Haskell penned a playful-but-condemning column, employing "conversation" from a personified, deeply offended Paul Bunyan statue, about Bangor Labor Day race organizers changing the traditional 2:00 p.m. start to 9:00 a.m. According to Haskell, the mythic, great lumberjack Bunyan was angry at having his early-morning slumber disturbed by the arrival of the runners and that traditions should not be so callously tossed aside, simply because heat and runner safety might occasionally be a concern. Spectators, too, were not appreciative of so early a start time. Haskell also quoted Hillgrove, who reportedly told him, "I couldn't believe they changed the time of that race to nine o'clock. I really couldn't. That race was starting at two o'clock before some of those runners were born. If people don't like the heat, don't run."

At the time, the author of this book and newspaper columnist Haskell had been friends for several years; as members of the 121st Public Affairs Detachment, Maine Army National Guard, I was the editor of the statewide newspaper for guardsmen, and Haskell was the paper's principal reporter.

I tried to write an equally lighthearted-but-pointed guest column for the newspaper, defending the new starting time. In very recent memory of these articles, a Down East runner had died as the result of heatstroke; further, spectators were still rather sparse for the event and hardly of consequence. I specifically noted that new, wonderful "traditions"—especially the presence of women—were developing that had been no part of the race's origins in 1963.

In a couple of paragraphs I intended as solely satiric, to mock ol' Paul's "be a man's man" chauvinistic attitude, I chided my friend Bob for not seeing and recognizing the new traditions to be appreciated. I mocked the failure to see how the sport was blossoming beyond just the elite runners.

I wrote, "what are all those old fogies and university professors, and bratty little kids and, goodness gracious, women—women of all things—doin' out there in the first place? Don't you have some knitting, Robin Emery? Back in the kitchen, Carol Roy! I want the race like it used'ta be, when men were—men!"

At a couple of races following publication of my column, Robin would see me, either at gathering areas pre- or postrace, or even while we were out racing the course, smile mischievously and say, "Knit—knit—knit."

Starting at the 1980 Bangor Labor Day 5-Miler, Robin Emery ran off a streak of seven straight victories, from 1980 to 1986, for the women's division, setting a new course record (her fourth) of 30 minutes, 20 seconds in 1981 and then, her fifth and final new course record, of 30 minutes, 12 seconds, in 1985 on the old, original *long* course.

In 1980, Robin ran the eighteenth Labor Day Race, winning for the seventh time in nine years. She took forty-third overall and ran 31:48.

In 1981, Robin the women's title for the second year in a row and eighth in ten years. She finished twenty-first overall, among ninety-nine, in that course record of 30:20.

The litany of *Bangor Daily News* headlines, expressing a sentiment that said essentially, "Yes, Emery won again" upset Robin; she wasn't at all pleased to be taken for granted. "Come on, now. Don't say 'Ho hum, Robin won another one.' These things aren't getting any easier, ya know," said the lady, directly to the newspaper reporter, who has become "the legend" of Bangor's 5-mile Labor Day road race. "You never know when some little kid is going to come along and beat you." She did add, about her victory, "I am *very* pleased. Another year down the tubes."

She'd done a 29:06 in another 5-Miler (the Portland Boys Club race) "but it has to be flat." The Bangor course is not flat. She did her first mile in 5:26 but then the course proved too difficult for her goal. The newspaper reported: She finished 2:29 ahead of next woman and thirty-seven places. She came home 1:28 faster and twenty-two places better than the previous year. She attributed her success to logging 3,600 miles a year.

In 1982, gunning for her ninth victory in eleven years, she won in 30:38, for twenty-ninth overall, eighteen seconds off the course record she set the year before. Her personal goal, of breaking thirty minutes on the course, wrote Bob Haskell, remained unfulfilled.

Haskell quoted her, "I can't break thirty minutes on this course," she said in mock disgust. "Every year I say I'm going to do it and I don't."

"When I got over there my watch said twenty-eight minutes," explained Emery, pointing to the far side of the half-mile track that the runners follow to the finish.

"I said, 'feet don't fail me now.' But I got into that sand and it seemed to be so long around." She won the race for third time in a row—and the next closest woman finished at 32:16.

For the 1983 event, the *Bangor Daily News* reported, "Gaige won't be able to defend. However, the queen of the Labor Day race, Robin Emery of Lamoine, will be back to defend the title she has won the past three years and nine of the last 11 Labor Days."

Emery won the women's half of the Northeast Harbor race in 30:28 and said she would be happy with a similar time on a more grueling Bangor course. "I'd be happy with anything in the thirty-minute range because of the hill (14th Street Extension) and the fact that the Bangor course is actually 5.2 miles," said Emery.

Emery told the newspaper that the Down East Striders had measured the course and discovered that it was two-tenths of a mile longer than had been advertised. "The fifth-grade teacher from Lamoine said she doesn't like being in the favorite's role but accepts it. When you're the favorite, everybody's out to get you," said Emery. "But what can you do?"

She intends to run the race same as she has in most recent years. "I used to try to go up the hill fast," explained the thirty-six-year-old Emery. "But now I slow down on it in order to save my oxygen and my legs. Once you get up the hill and onto the flat part, you can begin making up ten seconds a mile."

Larry Mahoney of the *Bangor Daily News* wrote the following in his account of the 1983 Labor Day race: "Anyone wanting to speak to the winners of the 21st annual Bangor Labor Day Road Race can kill two birds with one stone by going to the Bryant E. Moore Middle School in Ellsworth." That is where sixth-grade teacher Jim Newett and fifth-grade teacher Robin Emery spend the school year, right across the hall from each other, explained Mahoney, stating that "Emery coasted to her fourth consecutive women's title and 10th in 12 years with a time of 31:11. Old Town's Cynthia Lynch was second in 32:06. Emery . . . continued her dominance with another sparkling performance." She was thirty-ninth overall.

"I felt great," said Emery. "I felt like I was in control all the way. The course didn't control me. I ran the first mile in 5:20 and couldn't believe it. I took the hill slowly but was passing guys on it so I knew I was going to have a good race. I flew after that. If they [the other women] don't get me on the hill, they aren't going to get me." She said she was "very pleased" with her performance and said the time was a good one "considering the heat."

"I would have liked to have been a little closer to Robin but my time wasn't too bad," said twenty-three-year-old Lynch to Mahoney. "She went out in front at the beginning and stayed there. I thought I was catching her during the second and third miles but then she got stronger."

In the *Bangor Daily News* advance or "pre-write" article for the 1984 Bangor Labor Day race, the unnamed writer noted the following: Robin was identified by race director Bob Booker as the obvious favorite but he hoped a race might develop between her, Ann Blumer, and Cindy Lynch, none of whom had preregistered. Robin said of the race, "I'm happy to be alive at the end of it."

It was Newett and Emery, again, in 1984. Robin won the women's division in 30:39, more than thirty seconds faster than the victory the year before. It was her eleventh win in thirteen tries at Bangor.

Robin wins, again, in 1982.

In Larry Mahoney's race account for 1984, "If you missed the 1983 Bangor Labor Day Road Race, the 1984 version could have filled the void Monday. Newett and Emery win . . . but the weather was cooler and much more suitable.

"Emery had her hands full with Orono's Ann Blumer, who ran stride-for-stride with her until the Lamoine native pulled away on the downhill grade at West Broadway. Blumer finished second, 32 seconds behind. Blumer had beaten Emery to the finish line at the Winter Harbor Lobster Classic three weeks ago. Emery is 37 and Blumer is 29."

"She has gotten a lot better," said Emery about Blumer. "I've never had to race her before but today was different and it was a lot of fun. I had to run hard all the time."

The thirty-seven-year-old Emery had breezed to virtually all of her Bangor Labor Day victories, but she actually found herself trailing Blumer, who had beaten her at the Schoodic Point Race a few weeks before, following the long uphill stretch of the race that takes the runners from 14th Street Extension to Holland Street Hill to Wiley Street to Union Street. "I'm better running on the flat stretches," said Emery. "I don't like hills. Once I pulled ahead on West Broadway, I bailed the rest of the way."

"I had hoped I could lose Robin on the hill," said Blumer, who couldn't shake Emery and knew the race was over when Emery pulled away.

"Robin is a little stronger at this distance than I am and, once she pulled ahead, I knew I wasn't going to catch her," said the twenty-nine-year-old Blumer, a Midland, Michigan, native who obtained her master's degree in education from the University of Maine at Orono. "She was too good today." Blumer ran a 10K all-women's race in Augusta on Sunday, winning in 38:16.

"This is Robin's race," said Lynch, third place in 31:45. "She has won it so many times."

Emery said she wanted to extend her lead as much as possible just prior to the little hill leading up to the Bass Park oval "because I always die on that hill."

Robin and this book's author believe we share a special memory of *this* Bangor Labor Day race.

In those years we were frequently running close to the same pace, and I often saw the women's race-for-the-win developing out on the course. And in this instance, I had not expended too much energy in the first two miles and carefully negotiated the sharp inclines of the devilish third mile, with expedience and energy efficiency. After the hill on Union Street, I made the right-hand turn onto West Broadway ready to make an assault from there to the finish, in hopes of breaking thirty minutes on the course. And there, just as suddenly, with the exact same intentions—was—Robin Emery.

As Robin says, there are those "rare times when you feel like you're just flying. You feel like you're in the air—as much as you are on the ground." We began passing people, and most of West Broadway turned into kind of a game of tag: First, I was ahead—and then Robin was ahead, punch and counterpunch. There had actually been one woman (Blumer) *ahead* of Robin—and we both blew right past her. Soon, we'd outdistanced everyone in sight. We made the turn on Buck Street and sped the gentle downhill to reach Main Street. We were still, individually, locked right on the prize, hardly aware of each other anymore and now fighting to stay in contention with our only enemy, the relentlessly tick-ticking clock.

By the time we were on the racetrack, Robin had pulled well away from me. I've never handled well the sight and the smell of horse or cow droppings, and the multiple piles of horse droppings to be skirted had me doing my known-well-to-the-amusement-of-my-friends, dry-heaving routine. Neither of us broke thirty minutes, but we'd both broken thirty-one minutes, and we were both well satisfied with the effort, having set personal bests for the race. And today, I treasure the memory far, far more than the result. *(Author's note: I ran 30:56, with only Bill Pinkham and Greg Hildreth between Robin and me.)*

For the 1985 race, the course had a new finish line, "shortened" to an actual five miles by eliminating circling the actual racetrack. It finished in the parking lot immediately adjacent to the racetrack grandstands, and it was officially certified, by the Down East Striders Track Club, as a five-mile course. Robin Emery set her fifth course record, winning the event in 30 minutes, 12 seconds, for her sixth straight win and twelfth victory in the race.

She won the 1986 event, in 30 minutes, 29 seconds, for a staggering seventh straight victory in the race. The streak ended in 1987 when rival Cindy Lynch won the race, in 29 minutes, 43 seconds.

When Robin Emery won the 1988 Bangor Labor Day 5-mile race, in 31 minutes, 23 seconds, it meant she had captured the event fourteen times in seventeen years, dating back to her original appearance in 1972.

Because of marriage in the mid-1980s and a move to Massachusetts, Robin did not regularly return to the race until the late 1990s.

In the meantime, the old race muddled along, attracting its seventy or eighty attendees and rarely bringing in runners from around the state. It hardly made any sense to attend it unless you lived somewhere reasonably close by in the central Maine region. And then any runner the least bit familiar with the race had to consider the safety issues.

The author of this book had not only written guest commentaries for Maine's daily newspapers but frequently had contributed free articles for *Mainely Running*, a statewide publication created by Bob Booker and later, Roy "Chuck" Morris. On occasion, I would address the matter of the "fall from grace" Maine's second-oldest road race had experienced.

It was pretty obvious why so few runners made any effort to attend. The original governing agent for the race, the Bangor Parks and Recreation Department, now routinely put on the event as if it were an annual nuisance to be tolerated for one day and then forgotten about. And the failure to work with the Bangor Police Department and provide even a modicum of traffic control for the race route's many four-way, major thoroughfare intersections meant safety was of no concern to anyone in the area. I had regularly come to dub the event "The World's Most Dangerous Road Race."

One year, in the mid-1990s, Skip Howard and I found ourselves separately driving around the course while the race was in progress. We determined that if the race organizers and the Bangor police weren't going to do anything about safety, then we would. We started playing hopscotch, one individual going to a four-way intersection, playing traffic cop and holding up traffic while first the leaders sped through and then large groups of middle-of-the-packers, featuring any number of individuals hopeful of winning various age-group awards, made their way through the intersection, their progress uninterrupted by traffic. That individual would stay there, seeing through as many runners as possible—then abandon the post, hopscotch past the next intersection where the other "ad hoc traffic cop" had taken up a position, and get ahead of the leaders at the next dangerous intersection. We were enjoying the race, and we were relishing the opportunity to make an important difference in providing a safe course and uninterrupted travel for those hoping for prizes or fast times.

At one point, a Bangor patrolling officer stopped and warned us we were not "authorized" to do what we were doing. We acknowledged the warning—and kept right on taking intersections.

A couple of years later, Fred Merriam, the president of the central Maine-based Sub 5 Track Club, and I were asked if we would be willing to meet with Mike Lucas, now the Bangor Parks and Recreation Department director, concerning the future of the Bangor Labor Day Race.

He began our meeting by relating how much he had enjoyed watching the race as a young boy and how bothered he was by its obvious decline. He knew that we were both harsh critics of the race, and he did not dispute our reasons for being so. But, he wondered, if he were willing to do whatever it took to fix things and change the environment, would we help him? Essentially, the concerned Mike Lucas reasoned, we could continue to condemn—or become part of the team that could lead to the solution.

Mike saw Fred as the man who could come in and direct the race and make all the necessary changes to it structurally, to make it the best race it could be, while he made sure a new relationship was brokered with the Bangor Police Department to ensure that the race was as safe as it could possibly be. He saw me as the man who could help find ways to celebrate the race's history and bring back a prominence it should never have forfeited. He left these possibilities to us to discuss on our own and then get back to him.

Fred and I "bought" right into Mike Lucas, and we set immediately to the task. Mike was as good as his word and a number of our suggested changes were immediately implemented. Since the original course had already been altered, we decided that there was really no reason to "finish" the race in a parking lot and Mike agreed to let us have the race finish right in front of the Recreation Department building, less than a couple hundred yards down Main Street from the Paul Bunyan statue. That way we could use the building's gym for an awards ceremony (and to get out of inclement weather), and for restroom facilities.

Fred and I had the idea for recognizing the race's great performances and performers, and working with Mike we came up with the idea of "retiring numbers" in ceremonies where we brought back past champions or celebrated performers. We would present them with plaques and designate a number that was theirs and theirs only should they desire to come back and run the race again; it would be retired forever when they stopped attending the race. We all agreed that none of these individuals should ever have to pay again to enter the race.

We implemented that program immediately, in 1997, hosting Dave Farley, who'd won the race the first two years it was ever held. We had a plaque for him and gave him "#1" and we were off and running, creating a very new vibration for the race. The next year, 1998, we had all-time male race champion Bob Hillgrove (seven victories), who received retired "#2" and then—of course—we recognized Robin Emery with retired "#3" in 1999, following her incredible fifteenth victory in the race.

Fred and I agreed that we would keep the retired numbers program special—very exclusive—and not just routinely find a reason to make it an annual occasion. We were both quite shocked when Mike Lucas interrupted our awards ceremony the year following Robin's ceremony, when we had not planned to make a presentation, to retire two more numbers: "#4" for Fred and "#5" for me.

Now a deserving member of the Maine Running Hall of Fame, Fred Merriam died in 2004 of a brain tumor, but the difference he made in popularizing running all over central Maine for several decades makes him wholly fitting of such recognition. While I know Mike was aware of and appreciated the Bangor charity race (promoting local cancer research) I had created, the Terry Fox 5K, I remain humbled by this recognition and genuinely regard myself as the individual who probably should have not received so great an honor. Today, I can still "see" kindly Mike Lucas's face, exhorting us to join him and help restore the Bangor Labor Day Race to prominence. I'm so glad he reached out to us.

So Robin Emery had her special moment of recognition at the Bangor Labor Day Road Race, but she had one more special surprise to add to her never-to-be-equaled-or-surpassed legacy at the race—and no one was more surprised by this outcome than—Robin herself.

In 1998, she came to the race well past those glory times when she could run a six-minute-flat pace and compete for overall women's champion laurels. Now, she was well into Masters competition and hoping to claim an age-group award, running a seven-minute-plus pace. With a large group of runners at the starting line, it was impossible to tell who might be the early leaders that day and Robin set off, in the midst of the pack, with no illusions of grandeur and only hoping to defeat any older women she might encounter in the latter stages of the event.

She remembers seeing her old friend, Skip Howard, enthusiastically encouraging her, but she couldn't make out what he was saying to her. "I was running along and Skippy was there and he was yelling out 'Go, sweetie or honey (or whatever term of endearment he had for me)' I was winning—but I did not know that."

Today, Robin says, "Oh, *that* was the most thrilling of all the Labor Day wins because, one, I didn't expect it and, two, it was amazing that someone this old could do this! It was totally pouring rain that day and my friends, who taped the TV segment (she had to return to Massachusetts) called it 'the Win for the Aged' not 'the Win for the Ages.' I took the trophy down to my principal in Norfolk, Massachusetts and said, 'Look at this!' And I added, 'Can you believe it?!' And he was a nice guy who knew I ran, and all the people at the school were happy for me. They all thought it was amazing that I could win the race."

What does this record of achievement mean to her? "Well, the times—they are not bad. And to do it year after year—that is what is kind of amazing when you think about it."

The trophy for the overall women's winner of the race was already named in her honor. It was an extraordinary treat to see Robin accept the trophy, named for her, at the 1998 awards ceremony.

And, today, every year Robin still enjoys running through the race and then presents the Robin Emery Award to the overall women's division champion. In her typical self-effacing style she cracks, "Well, at least it's not the Robin Emery Memorial Trophy."

And in 1999, it was the author of this book who proudly presided over the ceremony to officially "retire" a number in Robin's honor, "#3," and present her a plaque, with a female figure affixed to it, celebrating her fifteen years of victories.

SIX

If You're a Runner, You Have to Run Boston—You Have to Do It!

IT WAS THE MID-1970S, with the "Running Boom" blossoming all over America, and new races were inaugurated and developing into annual events. America's interest in the marathon, the original 24.5-mile endurance race (expanded into the present-day 26.2-mile distance at the Olympics in 1908) that had been the signature event of the ancient Greek version of the Olympics and remained the most celebrated event—it was always conducted as the very last competition—of the modern Olympics, was also growing.

This national interest was surely piqued by American Frank Shorter's victory (last won by an American, John Hayes, at that historic 1908 marathon) at the Munich Olympics of 1972 and most certainly grew with then-unheralded New Englander Bill Rodgers's surprising, record-breaking run at the 1975 Boston Marathon. The diminutive, charismatic Rodgers would go on to capture the 1978, 1979, and 1980 Boston Marathons, putting him into second place to this very day, all-time, for the most wins at the world's oldest, continuing annual marathon.

And, as all Maine running enthusiasts know, extraordinary Cape Elizabeth schoolgirl Joan Benoit had blossomed into one of America's top female runners, confirmed when she won the 1979 Boston Marathon, further affirmed when she won the 1983 Boston Marathon in record time, and made immortal when she won the first-ever women's marathon at the 1984 Olympics.

So it that something akin to the siren's call to run a marathon came to Robin Emery. But not just any marathon. It had to be the Boston Marathon. She would determine to pass on the history she was building at Maine's oldest road race, the Portland Boys Club, and go instead, on Patriots' Day, to the Boston Marathon in both 1978 and 1979.

"If you're a runner, you have to run the Boston Marathon. You have to do it," she will say today, laughing but entirely earnest. Having read the books on the historic race had inspired her, and she was also aware that the race's popularity had demanded that the Boston Athletic Association, which had first created the race in 1897 (to better "prepare" its members for future Olympiads, after introduction to the event during the recently concluded, resurrected "Modern Olympics" of 1896), had set qualifying standards, for both men and women. For women, Robin would have to run a three-hour, thirty-minute debut marathon to be admitted into the 1978 Boston Marathon.

Robin elected to run the 1977 Marine Corps Marathon, held in November, to be run on what she was told was a basically pretty flat course. A number of running college instructors from the University of Maine at Orono, including Dr. Frank Roberts, were targeting this fall marathon and that helped Robin make her decision. Working off her regularly maintained base mileage of sixty or more miles per week, she expanded the program only slightly. She remembers, "Well, my mom thought I was gonna die because I was doing these twenty-mile training runs. I was trying to build my confidence, and I'd really come to determine that if I could run twenty miles I could do the last six miles."

Her old adversary—nerves—were a major issue before the race. She was very uncomfortable with the huge crowd and the anticipation of the unknown. She'd found a Marine to pass along her sweatpants to, asking him to hold on to them so she could retrieve them at the finish line. But then there was the waiting. Standing in this enormous crowd. And even when the starting gun was sounded Robin felt extraordinary anxiety as the sheer numbers of runners, not moving, lined up in front of her left her feeling helpless: "You wait. You're not moving."

Once she was out on the course, her natural instincts and her ability took over. She eased around the largely flat course. "It was funny because this is the 1970s and we're running by all these beautiful monuments . . . but at one point, a guy yells out 'That's it, that's the Watergate building.' It was, of course, a big deal then."

She enjoyed the vacation from intimidating Maine hills. In 1982, the author of this book would run the Marine Corps Marathon, looking for a relatively flat course to try to register his first sub-three-hour marathon, and I would be running in the midst of a group of runners who kept "psyching" themselves to "be ready" for the test of an upcoming hill that they all were fearing. Well, after we had approached the Capitol, passed beyond and were moving along another long, flat stretch, I innocently inquired, "When's *that hill* coming up?" Incredulous, they all whirled around at me in disbelief and one uttered, "We DID it!" And it was then that I realized these flatlanders considered the small grade up and around the Capitol as something formidable to be soberly approached and respected.

Robin was surprised at how easily she handled the final six miles. She was past the finish line, sitting on a bench without her sweatpants and suddenly she came completely, emotionally unglued.

She remembers, "So, I realized I had lost my sweatpants, and I burst into tears sitting on this bench. This was uncharted territory for me, the marathon. I'd run twenty miles, but never twenty-six. I'm sitting on his bench with Dr. Roberts, and I started bawling my eyes out, NOT because the sweatpants were missing but because it was just such a relief that it was over. I made it. I did it. Dr. Roberts was nonplussed with this crying woman; he did not know what to do."

Robin recalls that she "just got on the plane to go back, totally wiped out." She would write to the race director, asking if he could send her the commemorative race jersey because these were only available after the race and Robin hadn't known to pick hers up. He not only sent the shirt but informed Robin that she got fifth place among women, in her thirty-to-thirty-nine age group.

Robin was timed in 3 hours, 30 minutes, 43 seconds. She placed eleventh among the 125 women in that field of 2,800. She told Bob Haskell of the *Bangor Daily News*, "I felt better the last six miles than the first part of the race. Women don't seem to have as many problems with marathons as men do. Climbing Katahdin is harder for me than running a marathon."

The only issue remaining was whether she had qualified for the Boston Marathon, having run forty-three seconds over the three-hour, thirty-minute qualifying time. But because of the start, where she had clearly lost a couple of minutes just passing the starting line, Robin was ultimately ruled eligible to participate.

However, putting her anxiety about running and completing her first marathon in the rearview mirror did nothing to lessen her growing anxiety about running the Boston Marathon.

"Finishing the Marine Corps Marathon only meant that, now, I could start worrying about Boston. 'Am I going to get injured?'" (She had a little ITB syndrome developing but "I skied on it all winter anyway!") "'Will the weather be bad?' 'Will they accept my time because it really wasn't a 3:30?'" (They did, of course). "'Am I going to get down there okay?' and I was a mess," Robin recalls.

A surprising development, coming from her parents, took one of the questions out of the mix. "My mom said, 'Are you sitting down? We're going to go with you. Dad will drive you down.' I said, 'Oh, *thank you!* That will be great.'"

So her parents drove her to Boston and, by her own admission, "I was a wreck." When they entered the Prudential Building, then the headquarters for runners coming to Boston, to get her number, she actually encountered a man who knew her by name. There weren't *that* many runners and nowhere near the tens of thousands that were to come in the decades to come. Her number was only 300.

It helped, greatly, that Robin and her parents hooked up with veteran Maine runners Bill and Wendy Sayres, with Bill running the event and Wendy spectating, who toured the greater Boston area with them. They took pictures of Robin and "helped the neophyte Emerys who did not know their way around Boston" at all. Ultimately, they dropped her off in Hopkinton because, "in those days, there were no buses" transporting the hordes of runners from the finish line area at Copley Square in downtown Boston to the starting line.

Finally, it was time to run. She saw the legendary costumed runner known as "Cow Man" (he wore a rawhide running kit with a robust set of cow horns atop his head), and, for a time, she recognized and was right behind the two gentlemen who wrote the book on the Boston Marathon that she had read. When she reached the halfway point, at Wellesley College, "this guy in front of me went around twice," clearly over-relishing the attention the runners—the male runners—were receiving from the traditional gathering of the Wellesley College young women, who annually scream their lungs out on both sides of the barriers in front of their campus. "These women enjoy cheering for the men, but they go positively ballistic when they see a woman running," Robin remembers.

And, if the reader hasn't yet begun to recognize how unique, how extraordinary a person and a runner Robin Emery is, perhaps THIS revelation will seal the deal. Here's how Robin assesses her first face-to-face meeting with the legendary Heartbreak Hill.

"So, I was at the top of Heartbreak Hill and a cop said to me, 'Congratulations! You made it up Heartbreak Hill.' And I said to him, '*THAT* was Heartbreak Hill?' You know, those hills are like interstate hills, and they are NOT like the hills all through the state of Maine," she says, in all earnestness.

The history of the Boston Marathon is replete with the often sad, occasionally tragic consequences of the race being won between miles seventeen and nineteen, the feared three consecutive hills through Newton (which, it turns out, is the community along the route runners do the most miles in; the city of Boston, ironically enough, only comprises two miles of the route). It was legendary *Boston Globe* editor and writer Jerry Nason who was responsible for the nickname, in his account of the 1936 race when two legends dueled throughout the race, Johnny Kelley and Ellison "Tarzan" Brown, the Narragansett Indian from Rhode Island. Brown was leading the race moving up this third hill of Newton when Kelley overtook him and made the major mistake of patting him on the back, offering a moment of compassion for his rival, believing he was about to take control of the race. Brown responded by shifting into another gear, racing easily to victory and leaving, according to scribe Nason, Kelley "heart-broken" in his wake.

Every year both veteran and rookie participant, both skilled and less-skilled runner, all make the mistake of enjoying the early flat and often downhill topography of the course to arrive at these three hills in too weakened a condition to successfully race or even jog this section of the course. Spectators here offer encouragement but, once the elite runners have passed, even outstanding competitors who have miscalculated their race can be found walking Heartbreak Hill. Once the middle of the pack and the ones who will complete the marathon in four hours or more arrive, the hill is frequently littered with defeated walkers. Yes, Robin Emery is right that the hill itself isn't extraordinarily formidable BUT the timing of having three uphills in a row, with this one as the last to be negotiated, makes it *most* runners' nightmare.

So, Robin is past Heartbreak Hill—and now, it turns out, this Robin is ready to fly!

She recalls, "Every marathon I've ever run I fly over the last six miles. I fly because I'm so relieved it's over. You can just go, and I started passing people on Commonwealth Avenue [through Brookline and up into Boston's Kenmore Square]. In those days the crowds were like *this* close to you, and they're screaming in your ears. And I made the turn on Hereford Street and down the hill and into the Pru(dential)" building.

Robin located her parents, and her mom accompanied her inside to retrieve her bag. She says, "All these women's bags were in a pile; there weren't that many of us. And all around us there are guys who are sick . . . and screaming in pain. And cursing. And throwing up into the plants. And my mom—she KNEW running was bad for you—and she's whispering to me, 'THAT man is *crying* . . . and THAT man is—' And I said to her, 'It's okay, mom, we'll leave.' And we went back to our room where we found Vern (*Maine Sunday Telegram* columnist Putney) and did an interview. And then we drove back to Maine, and I remember being in the back seat, trying not to die."

At age thirty-one, Robin was one of 227 women at the 1978 Boston Marathon, one of thirty-seven Mainers to participate. She ran 3 hours, 29 minutes. At first she didn't know her time, she told the *Bangor Daily News*, "I was so excited at the end I forgot to look at my watch."

She added, "I kept my pace most of the way. The people on the way make it so great. There wasn't any hard part. I just enjoyed the whole thing."

Her second Boston, the 1979 Boston Marathon, was, in her words, "not as good as the first one. I read all the books about the lure of Boston—the lake that Tarzan Brown went in, Heartbreak Hill, the people who stand in the same spot, with their lunches." Gayle Barron won the 1979 Boston Marathon women's division, in 2 hours, 44 minutes, 52 seconds. Robin ran 3 hours, 35 minutes, 20 seconds, finishing 144th in the women's division, out of 184 women.

For that second appearance at Boston she followed the advice of those who told her she should wear a jersey with the name "Maine" on it so people could call out encouragement. Running pretty close to the same time again, she simply states, "It was just not as great as the first time." It was a little drizzly that year, and she wore sweatpants and, later, determined that she didn't need to return to Boston ever again.

In 1980, just prior to running Portland's Casco Bay Marathon, Robin told a Portland newspaper writer this about her Boston experiences: "Boston was such a mob scene. Last year it took me six minutes just to cross the starting line. You had to walk. I have a love/hate thing with marathons. I love it when it's over, but it's so hard to get all the training miles in." In an advance story for the Portland newspapers, the headline read "Casco Bay: Beaulieu and Emery favored."

The story further noted that when Robin Emery of Lamoine began running fifteen years before, Kim Beaulieu of Standish was only nine years old. At the time of the marathon Robin was thirty-four and Kim (who returned to her birth name of Moody after a divorce a few years later) was twenty-four.

Robin's best Boston was two years ago (1978), a 3:24, but of that performance she told Joanne Lanin of the Portland papers, "I started slow, and found I had plenty left at the twenty-mile mark. It was that way for all three marathons. I've never gone as fast as I can, so I'm just going to go out and do seven-tens and see what happens."

Robin shows her Maine pride at Boston in 1979.

And it was at that 1980 Casco Bay Marathon that Robin would run her best marathon, completing it in 3 hours, 03 minutes, and finishing fourth overall for women. Running with her friend, Steve Palley, the thirty-seven-year-old Emery remembers:

"I felt like I could go at any time." Indeed, admitting "it wasn't nice," she left Palley when she recognized, "I was ready to go. It was just one of those days: You feel like you can accelerate at any time. You don't get tired. I was not sore after that race at all; it was just the peak." This would be her fourth—and last—completed marathon.

A New Hampshire woman, Robin Snyder, won the women's division, with a time of 2 hours, 54 minutes, 05 seconds, taking seventy-seventh place overall and beating 1979 women's winner, Patricia Swenson's record time of 3 hours, 02 minutes, 39 seconds. Another New Hampshire woman, Karen Miles, was second, in 2 hours, 56 minutes, 12 seconds. Kim Beaulieu took third place, in 2 hours, 57 minutes, 34 seconds. And Robin was officially fourth, in a time of 3 hours, 03 minutes, 35 seconds.

Robin returned to the 1981 Casco Bay Marathon but dropped out on a cold and windy day. Turning into that wind left Robin in a state of mind completely unfamiliar to her. A group of friends were following her progress on the course and she found herself thinking "if I see them again, I'm quitting." She wistfully recalls: If I hadn't seen them I know I would have kept going . . . but I had told myself I'd quit. And there's a picture of me coming in and I'm quitting. You never know. The only time in my life that I've quit a race . . . and I hated myself for the whole year after that.

Robin entered that second Casco Bay Marathon believing she'd experience the same feelings and run the same way she had the previous year. She recalls, "I was right near [eventual overall women's division winner] Kim Beaulieu and I tried to stay with her—and that was a mistake. I wore myself out after we turned into the wind. BUT I should've kept going."

After running and completing four marathons, from 1977 through 1980, Robin recognized that the marathon might be her distance, but that it simply required so much training and—with her commitment to teaching—she did not have the time for it.

"It was so easy. I don't know why," she said. "It could be my event and I'd like to try, but I just don't have the time to train."

Today, she has no regrets about not having run more marathons. Robin states, Marathoning requires too much out of your life, too much training. All year. To run in the Boston Marathon, you have to run in the winter. You need to do those twenty-milers. Build up to it. And if you do a fall marathon, then you need to train through the summer, in the heat. Besides I was right around the edge of getting injured most of the time. Right on the edge of getting sick. Freezing all the time. Always hungry. Nah, I decided, I don't need it. NOW, I do think it was all right to do it. But 10Ks might be more my speed.

SEVEN

Winning Is Not a "Ho-Hum" Easy Thing at All

HAVING RUN FOUR MARATHONS as almost just a minor diversion, Robin Emery turned thirty years of age in the mid-1970s and entered a golden period of running races in Maine, extending to the end of the 1970s and lasting right through to the mid-1980s.

She had separated amicably from Rick Voelker in the early 1970s, securing a no-fault divorce decree a few years later, allowing her to resume her family name. She and her retired parents were now settled comfortably into what was once the Emery family summer home in Lamoine, completely winterized for their year-round use. She was wholly satisfied with her fifth-grade teaching job at the Moore School in nearby Ellsworth. And, now, she was able to run year-round, mixing in golf and biking in the summer with skiing in the winters.

After having now run for more than a decade, Robin was reeling off win after win at road races all around the state of Maine, in some cases beating her competition by two-, three-, and even four-minute margins while establishing streaks at a number of these races where she had never been beaten.

Entering this period she'd told *Maine Sunday Telegram* writer Lloyd Ferriss, in December of 1976, "Robin Emery derives such a high from racing that she'll sometimes return to a race scene the next day so she can run alone over the empty roads and 'hear the echoes.'" At the time she'd recently turned thirty and told Ferriss her interests included photography and the guitar.

"Sometimes when there's a teachers' meeting after school I'll find myself looking out a window watching the sky grow dark, wishing everyone would finish up so I can get out on the roads. That's when I train for racing, after school."

She added, "I especially like running in the fall because it's cool, although I must say that there is nothing like those summer evenings when it's about seventy and everything's still and you're running along and all of a sudden you just start flying. There's something about those summer evenings. I don't even breathe hard. It's like hitting my pace all of a sudden. I don't know what you call it, but it's nirvana."

However, prerace nervousness still plagued her and her relatively new-found athletic "celebrity" was only adding to her misery. She hated being *expected* to win, and she began to grow more and more irritated with sports writers who thought it was something *easy* to do because of the relative ease with which she was winning race after race.

"Racing's different," she told Ferriss. "In a way I hate racing because I get so uptight it's awful. I can't eat. I get sick before a race thinking about it and I just wish it were over. . . . But there's something special about being out in that long line at the start. The gun goes off and you run until you feel like you're going to die. And when it is over there just isn't anything like it. You feel good for days afterwards."

Yes, she says, her nervousness was worse than ever. "You don't know who is coming up. Joanie [Benoit], thankfully, was in Boston then. But it was worse than ever before—'cause who knows what little kid is going to come along and wipe you out! Trouble was when you win, people expect you to win again. I had to tell Bob Haskell [the *Bangor Daily News* reporter who frequently wrote about how easily her wins seemed to be achieved], 'You have to stop this—It's not ho-hum. You don't know what this is like.'"

Yet, interestingly enough, there were times when she harbored Olympic thoughts.

She remarked to Ferriss, "At thirty maybe I should be satisfied with what I've done, but I can't bring myself to say that I've come just so far and won't go any farther. Back there in my head I have Olympics fever bugging me. If they had a marathon or a 10,000-meter race for women I'd have to try. I'd take a year off from school to run." On this topic she told another reporter, "Sometimes I think I'd like to take a year off and see how good I could be if I just ran, slept, ran and ate. But you could go crazy thinking about it."

Ferriss was interested in any diet tips or training tips the thirty-year-old Robin Emery had for runners.

"If there's a secret to being a good runner it isn't in weird diets," she stated. "Some people go around advising carbohydrate overload or macro-biotic diets. But I've lived thirty years on my mother's cooking, and I'm a runner and healthy, so eat and be damned. As Dorothy Hamill [US Olympic ice-skating champion] once said, 'Without ice cream, what's fame?'"

And she told Ferriss, her mantra of running every day remained intact: "The most important thing is training every single day of the year. It isn't that hard because when you're hooked you never want to miss a day. Last year I had to miss some training because I broke two toes. It was awful. I felt fat. I had headaches. After two days, I hobbled out and ran. Weather never keeps me from training. Near here [Lamoine] there's a place called 'The Chute' where it's open to the wind and in winter the chill factor sometimes must be twenty below. I'll run out there feeling wonderful. I'll think of the race season coming up in the spring and know that somewhere there's someone who skipped training that day. I've got an edge on that runner."

Turning thirty hadn't meant settling for some of those newly inaugurated age-group awards, though she picked up several of those along the way. Robin remained dominant, especially at central and Down East races that had suddenly sprung up. She frequently not only held the course record but had a streak of victories that was unbroken since her first appearance.

At this time she regarded her three best race performances as: 1977, Bonne Bell mini-marathon (10K), twelfth out of 2,800 women, in a time of 37 minutes, 14 seconds; 1977 Bangor Labor Day 5-Miler, 30 minutes, 12 seconds, as first woman; and 1975 New York Central Park 10K, seventh out of 300-plus women, 37 minutes, 43 seconds.

In 1978 Robin won the Maine's Female Runner of the Year, winning eleven of twelve races, losing only to Joan Benoit in the Olympia 5-Miler ("I'm automatically second whenever Joanie's around"). In the Bonne Bell Race held in Boston she finished twentieth out of 4,500 women (a race also won by Benoit).

Writing in an article published in 1985, runner and first individual to publish a magazine solely devoted to the Maine running scene, Rick Krause could already credit Robin for two very special legacies: "So longevity is one thing Emery can lay claim to. What about success? One entry form gave it all away. Tucked in the middle of *Maine Running* magazine is an entry blank for the Harbor House 5.5-Miler in Southwest Harbor. Listed are the men and women's winners since '79. For the men, the list goes Howland, Westphal, Gaige, and Fredericks. For the women it's Emery, Emery, Emery, Emery."

Rival central Maine runner Carol Weeks remembers, "When I started running in the late 1970s while living in Bangor, there were only two other women who lived near me that were runners, Barbara Hamaluk and Robin. Barbara lived in Bangor and was a great role model for me; she invited me to go with her to the Mardi Gras Marathon in New Orleans. This was my second marathon and both Barbara and I qualified to run in the Boston Marathon in 1979. My memories of Robin are mostly from entering many races and learning from her about how to be a tough competitor. I remember the close relationship that she had with her dad and how he would go with her to all of her races. I found this to be very cool. I observed how much he enjoyed watching her compete and his loyal support of her racing. They were inseparable, which in some ways prevented me from getting to know Robin better. Robin was both strong and fast. She raced smart, always holding enough in the tank to finish strong and usually in first place. Although I never trained with Robin, I have always respected her and hold her in the highest regard."

Robin already had victory streaks of five and six years and course records at most of her favorite races of this era, in addition to the Harbor House 5.5-Miler: Southwest Harbor 10K, Northeast Harbor 5-Miler, Tour du Lac 10-Miler, Bar Harbor 13.1-Miler, Hancock 10-Miler, Great Cranberry Island 5K, Hampden 8½, Epstein's 5K, as well as several annual races right in her hometown of Ellsworth, including Grand Willey, Autumn Gold, and Union Trust.

Highlights of her 1978 racing season in Maine included the following victories: Dyer Memorial 5K, new course record of 18:55; 10K in Auburn, in 41:56; Bangor Red Cross 10-Miler Road Race, 68:18; first Goldsmith's Women's 6.5-Miler, in 35:49; Hampden 8.5-Miler, in 58:46; Greater Bangor Open Invitational Track & Field Meet at U-Maine, where she won the 10,000-meter race in the morning (knocking nearly six minutes off the previous record), in 39:05, and the junior Masters mile in the afternoon; first annual Bar Harbor 13-Miler, in 1 hour, 27 minutes, 29 seconds (the next woman was more than ten minutes behind); ninth annual Elks Midi-Marathon, 1:22:26; and Cape Elizabeth 5.8-Mile Turkey Trot, in 34 minutes, 24 seconds, smashing her own course record of 36:57 in 1977.

One understands, fairly quickly, just how competitive Robin Emery is, yet she has another side that offers something you might not expect: respect for one's peers. She explains, "35 minutes, 40 seconds is my best 10K, which I set at the 1978 Bonne Belle race. But coming into the finishing stretch, I found Gayle Barron right in front of me. And I'm thinking to myself—remember this is the 1970s—I'm thinking to myself 'She's an Olympian, she's a marathoner and she's famous. I better not pass her; it would not be right.' . . . She's only a few yards in front me. I did think that; it entered my head." Some of this thinking, Robin believes, is because she still really had no understanding of race tactics. The course was basically flat but Robin admits she was continuing to wrestle with her nerves. Barron would win the 1979 Boston Marathon. Robin did not pass. Today, Robin has her Bonne Belle bell from the race because they had just started passing out age group awards and she was in her thirties (she turned thirty in 1976). Bangor's Labor Day race and other Maine races started having age group awards in the 1980s.

Highlights of her 1979 season included the following victories: second annual 14-Miler Old Town Runners Classic, defending her title in 1:36:29, smashing earlier time of 1:39:29; Bangor Red Cross 10-Miler, in 1:03:40 (beating second place finisher, 1:08:45, and smashing time from year before, 1:08:18); first annual Great Cranberry Island 4.8-mile road race, in 30:17, with second place in over 32 minutes; Goldsmith's Second Annual Women's 10,000-Meter Race, 35:00, clipping forty-nine seconds off her course record a year earlier (second place was 1:19 behind); Harbor House (Southwest Harbor) 5.5-mile Fall Foliage, 32:52; second annual Bar Harbor 13-mile race, 1:28:52; fourth annual Tour du Lac, in Bucksport, in 65:07, bettering her course record by more than a minute and a half, set the previous year; Elks midi-marathon run in 1:24:58.

A portion of her 1979 campaign, including the Grand Willey 10K and the Bangor Labor Day Race, were adversely affected by a bicycle accident she had.

Robin remembers, "I found an old lobster buoy at the beach. I hung it on the handlebars. On the way home, the buoy caught in the spokes, and I went over the handlebars, landing on my face," breaking her glasses and requiring stitches. "The worst part was," she adds, "I had toe clips, so the bike went with me. I had horrible muscle spasms and could hardly walk or run for about two months." When she did run, such as at the 1979 Bangor Labor Day race where she posted a surprising third-place finish losing to a winning time of more than thirty-four minutes, "it still was hard to go all out. I really didn't get better until the following spring."

Her 1980 Patriots' Day comeback victory marked a full return after the bike accident. And by that fall, her 13-Miler win at Bar Harbor was her seventeenth win in nineteen starts. She was able to exult to veteran Portland newspaper writer Vern Putney that she now had some races in her own backyard. "I'm racing every weekend and saving tremendously on gas and sack time. With races concentrated in this area, I am not rising at dawn and hitting the highways for a prolonged stretch. This is most appreciated, perhaps on the return run. Postrace letdown and mental fatigue can set in."

The first female sports writer for *Bangor Daily News*, Joni Averill, occasionally did a column called "The Other Half" on females in sports and Robin was the focus of one of these columns during the summer; it was principally about how badly Robin wanted to win Grand Willey 10K, set for August 9, 1980.

Robin told Averill about how she never takes a day off, noting, "I run every single day. I'm a run-aholic. If I don't run, I don't feel well." She

Robin races to victory at the 1980 Grand Willey race, under the watchful camera eye of her father.

added, "Running keeps you sane. . . . After a run, you feel like you can put your head back on. It helps you approach anything from a teacher's conference to climbing a mountain with a clearer perspective of what you can achieve."

The then-thirty-three-year-old had won twelve of the fourteen races she had entered since April. But there was one race, she told Averill, that meant more to her than any of the others and that was the Grand Willey 10K in Ellsworth.

"I'm concentrating on that right now. I won't be running in any race until that one." The year before, she told Averill, she fell off her bike two weeks before the race and the effects of the accident were still lingering during the race. "I was really embarrassed. I came in third. The Grand Willey is my home turf, I wanted to win."

In 1980, Emery was definitely going to be the woman to beat, Averill proclaimed. "I'm just going to fly." At the age of thirty-three, she was proud to say that she was running strong. "I'm running not older but faster," she laughed. And it is a fact that "constantly improving" was what gave her satisfaction. She noted, of her third consecutive title at Goldsmith's 14-Miler, she was "really pleased . . . because I ran it six minutes faster than last year." She explained that she preferred cooler temperatures to summer's heat but, for Grand Willey, "I've made up my mind the heat will have no effect on me in Grand Willey!"

Robin was as good as her word: She won the Grand Willey 10K, in record time of 41 minutes, 15 seconds, on a very hot day. Other highlights of her 1980 season included the following victories: 5K Castine Eagle Road Race, 19:15; Bangor Athletic Attic 10K, 39:01 (second woman was 42:26); fifth annual Tour du Lac 10-Miler, 65:38; Southwest Harbor Memorial Day 5.7-Miler, 34:29; Bangor July Fourth 5K, 18:25; Great Franklin 10K, 36:09, shattering the early women's mark by over eight minutes (second place finished behind her by more than three minutes); second annual Great Cranberry Island 4.8-mile race, with a new record time of 29 minutes, 49 seconds; Dogwood Fun Run 5-Mile Race (Connecticut), 30:46 finishing thirty-second out of 453 finishers; Bar Harbor 13.1-Miler (using Acadia National Park's loop around Eagle

Lake for the first time), 1:24:33 (cutting more than four minutes off her previous best).

A comical memory the author of this book has of Robin occurred in the early 1980s at a one-time-only, five-mile race in Lewiston, sponsored by a bank. A group of us from the central Maine area traveled down to it, in one van. Robin was practically bouncing off the walls of the vehicle with anticipation and excitement. The reason: first prizes, for male and female, in the overall category, were $100 gift certificates to L.L. Bean! Usually, in races featuring a serious hill (like Montello Hill in this race), Robin raced upgrades conservatively. Not this day. She just "smoked" it and beat me and others of her traveling companions to the finish line by huge margins. Of course, she gleefully collected the gift certificate; the second place woman in the race was never any factor in the contest and finished far back of me.

Robin took third place at the Cape Elizabeth Turkey Trot, to Joanie and a woman from New York State; she ran 35:10 in the 5.8-mile Cape Elizabeth race. She finished the 1980 season with twenty-two wins in twenty-five races.

Highlights of her 1981 season included the following victories: Mad Witch half marathon, 1:27:54; Tour du Lac 10-Miler, 67:30; Hancock 10.2-mile race, in new course record of 1:07:30; Blue Hill 10K, 40:02.7; first Les Femmes d'Acadia, leading a field of 50 women and winning in a time of 45:16 on the nearly 7-mile course (second place finished in 51:40); Cape Elizabeth nine-mile race, 60:32; second-straight third annual Grand Willey, setting new women's course record in 40:01 (Andrea Hatch was second, in 43:56); fifth annual Southwest Harbor 6.2-mile race, 39:05; third annual Fall Foliage 5.5-mile race, in 33:30; Bar Harbor, in 1:25:44 (second woman ran 1:29:12); thirteenth annual Cape Elizabeth Turkey Trot 5.8-mile race.

At times she thought she might be racing too much. A writer found this amusing and noted that after winning a race on Saturday and complaining that she was "racing too much" she came back on Sunday to win the women's division of the Everybody Triathlon—a 2.6-mile run, a one-mile row, and a five-mile bicycle ride!

And occasionally she tried winning something other than a running event: She did the second annual Backside ten-mile bike race, finishing behind Marsha Giglio, in 30:49, in Southwest Harbor, with a time of 34:11. In her scrapbook, next to this result, she wrote to herself, "Stick to running!"

Winner of twenty-two races in 1981, Robin was named Maine Woman Runner of the Year by the Maine Runner's Association—the second year in a row she won the title and third time overall.

In a Bangor race created to attract elite runners from all over New England, Robin finished third at Benjamin's 10K, in 37:17.9, behind Joanie and Marjorie Podgajny.

Highlights of her 1982 season included the following victories: Spring Eagle Run 5K, Castine, 17:30; first annual Bangor Terry Fox 5K, 18:23; five-mile Moosebec Race (Jonesport-Beals); second annual Les Femmes d'Acadia race, for women only, in Southwest Harbor, 40:09, (second was 42:38); Union Trust 4-Miler, 25:10; seventh Tour du Lac 10-Miler, establishing a new women's course record, in 64:35 (breaking her own course record, 65:07); sixth annual Southwest Harbor 10K, in 38:49; Jonesport Sesquicentennial five-mile road race, in 30:44, (knocking almost seven minutes off the previous women's record!); third straight Grand Willey 10K race in Ellsworth, 39:23, breaking her previous year's record, 40:01; third annual Scott Taylor three-mile race, in 21:40; third straight in third annual Autumn Gold 20K in 1:22:28, for twenty-first overall (second was 1:28:46); Cape Elizabeth Turkey Trot, 34:24; Harbor House 5.5-mile Fall Foliage race in Southwest Harbor, 33:34; Castine Twosome, setting new women's division record, 31:36 (trimmed thirty-four seconds off the record); 13-Miler Bar Harbor, 1:25:51; Northeast Harbor 5-Miler, 28:42. (second place was more than four minutes later); 15.2-mile Mad Witch in Brewer, 1:43; 5-Miler Northeast Harbor, 30:16; Southwest Harbor Fall Foliage 5.5-mile, 32:44 (seventh overall and next woman was 38:58); Autumn Gold 20K race, 1:19:05.

At the 1982 Benjamin's 10K, Greg Meyers, who would go on to win the 1983 Boston Marathon, narrowly beat Maine's elite runner Bruce Bickford. Robin took third place, in a stellar 36:50, for seventy-fifth overall. Headed for her second Boston Marathon title in 1983, Joan Benoit Samuelson was first, in 32:43 and eighteenth overall; Karen Dunn, a nineteen-year-old who ran a world junior record for the marathon (2:34:33), was second, in 34:53, for forty-fourth place. Dunn said she wasn't in peak shape "but I know I'm not in her [Benoit Samuelson's] class. I saw her at the start and said 'good bye.'"

After the race, Robin was actually very happy. As she explained to Rick Krause, "Sometimes," she said, "I just like to be nobody. That's why at Benjamin's (10K in Bangor) I do so well. Because they don't expect me to do anything so I really do well. I got third behind Joanie and Dunn."

Earlier that summer, the organizers of the Bangor Fourth of July 3K found a novel way to keep Robin from winning, when a race official unintentionally directed her right out of the race. *Bangor Daily News* reporter Bob Haskell wrote that Cynthia Lynch of Old Town, thirty-third overall, was the women's winner in 10:43 after front-running Robin Emery of Lamoine was "misdirected down to the Kenduskeag Plaza parking lot and out of the race. Emery was not nearly as distressed by the heat as she was by the bad directions which detoured her and, she said, a couple of other runners down to the parking lot and under the new foot bridge where everyone else was finishing. 'I was winning it, man. But they told me to come down there, so I ran down there.'" Although she explained that she thought something was wrong, she did not fully realize the mistake until she crossed the little footbridge that connects the two parking lots and stopped running beneath the finish line on the new footbridge that everyone else was using.

In November of 1982, Robin's father died. She remembers, "I know I never had a more difficult time going for a run than the day after my father passed away. He had always taken an interest in my running. He would go with me to the races and take pictures. I didn't know if it was proper to be out running the next day. But my mom said, 'Go out. He is with you every step of the way.' It was hard to run with a lump in my throat, but I felt better afterward. I believe he would have wanted me to run that day."

Robin adds, "I dedicated a lot of my races in 1983 to him, especially the Boys Club victory in the spring."

In addition to that Boys Club 5-Miler, highlights of her 1983 season, included the following victories: first annual Frostbite 3.5-mile run for MS, 22:16; fourth annual Spring Eagle 3-Mile Run, Castine, 17:01; Northeast Harbor race; Southwest Harbor Days 10K on Saturday, 38:24; Scott Taylor Memorial 5K run, 21:41; third annual Les Femmes d'Acadia 6.5-mile race, in 42:45 (second was 45:52); fifth annual Great Cranberry Island 5K, in 18:11; third annual Union Trust 4-Miler, 24:38; Orono Boosters Club 5-Miler, 30:36; second annual Terry Fox 5K, in 18:01, for seventeenth overall, in a field of 530; Tour du Lac in 66:30, for twentieth place overall (Andrea Hatch was twenty-first, in 67:29); Bar Harbor 13-Miler,1:26:06; Autumn Gold 10K, 38:41, ten seconds off her winning time the previous year; sixth annual Fall Foliage 5.5-mile road race, in 33:10 for third place overall, winning this race in the women's division for the sixth time.

Robin has called the Great Cranberry 5K one of her absolute favorite events. It was called one of America's "25 most unique running events in US" by *Runner's World* magazine.

Competitors had to participate in a lottery to gain admittance. That was because the only way to reach the island was by ferry and there were only so many seats available and only two scheduled ferry rides the morning of the event. The lottery had nearly 600 applicants and an exclusive field of 300, with runners from twelve states and Canada. She enjoyed seeing her streak at the race extend to five straight victories.

And at the second annual Terry Fox 5K, her victory meant receiving a signed copy of Stephen King's latest novel, *Christine*, from the author himself.

She won twenty-two races in 1983 and had won seven times in 1984 at the time. She was in her seventeenth year as fifth-grade teacher at Moore School.

Robin was training under the direction of Steve Coffin, head track coach at Ellsworth High School. She cited that lifting weights and "intelligent pacing" were aspects of that training. She was running sixty-five to seventy miles a week, a long of fourteen miles and a shorter four-miler, faster, the next day. And she was varying her routes. This came about

Robin wins 1985 Portland Boys Club race.

because "I was getting depressed with all those young kids coming along. So I went to Steve Coffin and asked him if he could help me. He said I was going too fast for too many miles and was getting tired out. 'You don't need that much speed, you beat yourself into the ground.'" She started wearing heavy shoes to train during the winter—"When I put those [her racing shoes] on, I fly." And she was looking forward to turning forty in early October—"Only runners want to turn forty"—because it means she could start racing Masters' events.

Emery's biggest competitor during this period, was, simply, the clock. "It's fun to run against your own record." She was careful to never preach: "As a whole, Americans are pretty unfit. I try to set an example for my students, rather than preaching to them."

Highlights of her 1984 season included the following wins: Bar Harbor Police 5K, 18:09; Hancock Days Lobster Classic ten-mile road race, 1:06:25, with second place finisher, 1:09, and Robin nineteenth overall; Northeast Harbor 5-Mile Race, in 30:02, and twenty-seventh overall; Southwest Harbor 10K, 38:30; China 10K in record time, in 38:58, beating second-place finisher, who was 39:28 (written up in *Runner's World*)—and on her first visit to the race.

But it wasn't always about fast times and victories. One time she could even be talked into slipping off the roads, in the midst of a race, for a quick plunge into Silver Lake, while running Bucksport's formidable Tour du Lac!

Race veteran and longtime friend Skip Howard admits, "It was my doing, entirely, I confess. It was my idea, but Robin didn't need much urging, given the stultifying heat and the fact that, at that point in the race, Personal Bests were out of the question. You must remember those were the days when a PR was the principal goal."

He recalls, "As it turned out, Robin and I ran a similar pace, especially in the middle-distance 10K to half marathon events. It was at one of the early Tour du Lac 10-Milers in Bucksport that Robin and I found ourselves running stride for stride down the gradual incline toward Silver Lake."

Howard recalls that the race was held in "a sweltering late June, early summer heat wave," and "we were running at probably 6:30-minutes-per mile-pace early on. But, now, it was more likely seven-plus by that point. Today was *not* going to be a personal best for either of us. Having conceded as much, at least inwardly and probably aloud, I found myself assessing our current condition: We were already soaked from sweat, water stops, and use of on-course water hoses; our running socks and shoes were soaked and making squishing noises."

Howard: Man, Silver Lake looks really inviting.

Robin: Yes, very.

Howard: I can't wait to get back to camp for a swim.

Robin: I'm going to take an ocean dip when I get home.

(Silence, both runners drawing ever closer to the boat landing.)

Howard: Why wait? Let's go in the lake now.

Robin: What? Are you nuts? That'll mess up our finish time!

(Silence—and second reflection on that point leads her to far less concern about that finishing time!)

Robin: Oh yeah . . .

Howard: Yeah, just what I was thinking. So, ready, wanna go in?

Robin: I don't know. Seriously?

Howard: Watch me!

Robin: Me too!

Robin scored regularly in state and out of state all through the 1980s. Here she is after placing well, again, at the Bonne Belle, Boston, 1989.

Howard remembers, "Thirty seconds later, we're back running, refreshed, giggling, and laughing, body temperatures cooled for the last three miles or so of the race. And we were passing some runners, catching up to others. Robin might concur that our impulse was one of the smartest mid-race decisions we ever made. What a great time it was!"

EIGHT

Men for Whom It Was "One Big Damn Deal" to Beat Robin

MANY MEN, INCLUDING THE AUTHOR of this book, found Robin Emery to be more than someone to be admired as a skillful runner. She was an outright worthy adversary.

As I alluded to earlier in the book, I began running the Portland Boys Club Race in 1973, shortly after joining the Portland newspapers and starting graduate school at the University of Southern Maine. Though I began dreaming of running the Boston Marathon while I was an undergraduate at Northeastern University in the 1960s, in truth, I had never run an actual race over three miles and never gone any farther than seven miles at any one time. A stint at Army Basic Training in the summer of 1971 had revealed that I could run a mile in 5 minutes, 11 seconds wearing fatigue pants and combat boots, and best anyone in my forty-eight-member Charlie Company unit for any of our timed one- or two-mile runs. But that hadn't properly prepared me for that damn, lovely young lady who kept passing me, annually, early in the second mile of the Portland Boys Club race.

Every year, I joked, I would "train for the upcoming softball season," by getting into shape and running the Portland race. It makes me laugh recalling how I'd run five miles every day for two or three weeks, racing as hard as I could every workout—all of which made me fast enough to beat Robin for just that first mile.

It was only starting in 1978, when I first began training year-round and following two full seasons of racing experiences, that I enjoyed my "coming out" party as a worthy, properly trained runner of roads. Thanks to training regularly with Steve "Silver Fox" Norton and a number of other University of Maine at Orono professors and staff, I had started to finish ahead of some of central Maine runners I had admired. I had my list—and, one by one, I would have that "good day" and beat someone I'd never beaten before. Yet, I still—hadn't—beaten—Robin!

It was the summer of 1980 and a very hot day for the Grand Willey 10K in Ellsworth. On a very tough uphill, leading out of the downtown area and back to the finish line at the old middle school, I'd pulled ahead of Robin and kept working that hill, feeling like I was going to post a good, credible mid-thirty-minutes time. On the flatter stretches, Robin had caught and passed me. And she was ahead of me as we reached the school and a portion of the track to be run to cross the finish line.

I saw Robin just ahead of me and knew I felt strong enough to beat her to the finish line. I let what was left in the tank out and crossed the finish line ahead of her. I ran 41 minutes, 10 seconds, for forty-fifth place out of around 175 runners. Robin finished in 41 minutes, 15 seconds, setting a new course record for women.

When she crossed the line, I could not resist the urge to blurt out my accomplishment. I rushed over to her and with more excitement in my voice than I'd hoped with which to express myself I said to her, "That's the first time I've ever BEATEN you!" Yes, I immediately recognized what a complete jerk I sounded like—and apologized. To her credit, Robin just smiled and said, "No. it's okay—I don't mind—I'd only be *bothered* if a woman did that to me."

It was only all these years later, working on this manuscript together, that I discovered how important that race was to Robin; for this is the race, on her "home turf" of Ellsworth, where she'd finished third the year before following that terrible bike accident. She returned, vowing to herself not to be beaten again—and she'd won, with a new course record.

So, I am, most definitely, a card-carrying member of the Men's Club hankering to beat Robin—and joked about it—often.

Robin bests this author, Northeast Harbor, 1983.

And, oh yes, there are most definitely others. There's Skip Howard, who says he doesn't remember exactly where it happened but that it took him some time to match steps with her.

Recalls Howard, "I've talked with Robin about my very first recollection of her, when I was struggling to get to a half-hour jog." It was when he was the continuity director/copywriter at WLBZ-TV, Channel 2 in the early 1970s. The sports reporter had just returned from Lamoine with film and audio of a woman schoolteacher doing a very long run.

"Guys, you won't believe this! I just filmed a girl doing a fourteen-mile training run in Lamoine!" he said, almost in disbelief. Howard remembers, "I bolted from my typewriter" and raced into the adjoining office to see the footage.

Howard reflects, "I'm sure Robin was called 'a girl' then. In fact she was then, in the mid-'70s, a woman in her twenties, a schoolteacher, and already a dedicated athlete and very good golfer. For me, struggling to overcome the thirty-minute, three-mile barrier in my own attempt to become a runner, I found her fourteen-mile run to be jaw-dropping and revealing. As I watched the silent film footage of Robin running on the coastal roads and woods of her hometown, I was struck by the effortlessness of her strides. As I was soon to discover in the next several years, her gliding, fluid form belied the quickness of her leg turnover; in a five-kilometer race particularly, that fluidity was as admirable as the distance it would cover, while one was watching from further and further behind or being passed."

Bob Steele, WLBZ's sports director, married and edited a magnetic tape soundtrack to that footage (this before the news industry's advent of the newest technology, two-inch videotape) for that evening's broadcast, Howard recalls, adding, "As I watched the outtakes off and on during the remainder of the workday, I was inspired by Robin's accomplishment and her style. Observing her running form during the various outtakes of Bob's editing, I grasped the essence of pacing that was eluding me in my own training. Little did I know that within a few brief years, she and I would be running, often together, at many of the road races in the Eastern Maine region."

Robin notes that along with Skip Howard, veteran runners Vaughn Holyoke and Gerry St. Amand told her she had been "a target" for them to beat somewhere, finally, in a race. Her close friend, Tom Kirby, also readily admits to being a member: "I don't really remember the first time I beat Robin. I do remember years and years of chasing her."

Kirby, a frequent travel companion, notes, "I have to coax her to leave early when we travel together. I like to get to a race about an hour before; she likes to get there about a half an hour before. Normally I like to leave right after the awards; she likes to hang around until there's no one left to talk to. We've had some fun trips to Belfast and Rockland, especially those where we go to the Goodwill Stores. The last race I went to with her was the Healthy High 5K in Orono. While we were at the race there was a bad accident on Route 1-A. To avoid taking a detour we went into a restaurant—and by the time we were leaving and getting down near the spot a guy was just removing the cones and opening up the road again. We looked at this as going from Last to—First!"

According to his wife, the late Fred Merriam was a "member" in good standing. Joan Merriam recalls, "I remember when Fred first started racing, he wasn't aiming to catch or beat any particular guy. He felt that if he could summon the speed to finish ahead of Robin it would spell success. If I remember correctly, it took him a few years to accomplish that goal, and I believe he was not alone. I think a bunch of guys placed an imaginary target on Robin's back."

Indeed.

Notes Mike Carter, the outstanding runner from Machias, "Yes, I'm going back to the hard drive called a soft brain these days, but do remember how proud I was to finally catch, pass, and beat the Lovely Lady from Lamoine."

For her part, Robin alleged, speaking to Lloyd Ferriss of the *Maine Sunday Telegram*, back in December of 1976, "Racing is different for women than it is for men, even though we enter many races together. I don't always feel competitive against guys although some of them—especially the younger runners—feel competitive toward me. I don't know if women will catch the men in distance running. It may be too early to tell. I tend to think that good male runners will always beat good women runners, but the differences will get closer. But that's not why we're in it, to beat the men. There are right reasons and wrong reasons for racing, and if you're in it just for the trophies and competition you're in it for the wrong reasons. If you run because you want to be strong and feel good, then that's better."

Hmmm, not a big deal to beat men, huh, Robin? Well, it turns out there are *some* men it was a big deal to her to beat in a race.

In a 2015 *Ellsworth American* feature on her by Taylor Vortherms, Robin, discussing her first appearances at races around Maine, stated, "Most of the runners didn't have a problem with it, except for the ones who didn't want to get beat by a woman. Then war was declared on my part." Vortherms writes that, next, Robin . . . sighed . . . "wistfully" and then whispered to her, "I *loved* to beat *those* men."

NINE

Masters Running and Massachusetts Years, 1985–2000

ROBIN EMERY ROLLED ALONG in the early 1980s, comfortably mixing her life in the classroom with her life racing the roads in Maine. She continued using golf and skiing as a way to relax from competition.

She had no idea how *everything* was about to change just because of a visitor to her classroom.

Joseph Rappa was a curriculum consultant the Ellsworth school system had hired to come in, do an assessment, and make recommendations. Robin admits he initially made her quite paranoid, especially when he kept reappearing in her classroom, making her think he had concerns about her and what she was doing as a teacher.

And when he asked her out to dinner, she had worked herself into an internal frenzy believing this was just a polite way to tell her he was going to fire her.

It was only when they were at the Hilltop Restaurant in Ellsworth and the conversation remained completely relaxed and unrelated to her professional abilities that Robin finally saw a different possibility and meekly asked, "Is this a date?"

Indeed, it was.

Harvard PhD graduate and longtime Massachusetts educator Joe Rappa thought he might like a professional change of venue from the rat race of Massachusetts to the quiet, rustic place he envisioned Maine to be, but a person, rather than a place, had really caught his attention.

They married in 1985 but shortly thereafter Joe Rappa decided he wanted to return to Massachusetts, to take a position as a public school superintendent, in Avon. Though this had originally been a deal-breaker for entering into a marriage contract, reluctantly, Robin agreed to move with him.

By 1985, she had taught fifth grade at the Moore School in Ellsworth for eighteen years, teaching in the same room, the same school. "Don't quit your job," her mom wisely counseled. Robin agreed and arranged for a leave of absence, coming back to Ellsworth to complete twenty years in the state system and qualify for her pension. But, she acknowledges simply, "I promised things in marriage—so I had to move to Massachusetts."

"My mom knew all of this was a mistake—and she was right," Robin recalls. "They say opposites attract and that was certainly us." The sixteen-year relationship put them at odds frequently, Robin recalls, because Joe wasn't that interested in sports and felt the need to take control in all facets of his life, personal as well as professional. "I knew I wasn't in the right place when I was about to go off to a race, the Bar Harbor half marathon, and Joe said he didn't want me to go. He said we 'needed to talk,' but it turned out that he just didn't want me going off to race."

The couple originally moved so Joe Rappa could become a school superintendent for the school system in Avon, but then he accepted the Attleboro, Massachusetts, school superintendent post. At first, Robin was hired to be a gifted and talented teacher in Pembroke, but subsequently she was hired to be a fourth grade classroom teacher at Norfolk Centennial Elementary School. The couple found a home and moved to Bridgewater, Massachusetts.

What did work out beautifully for Robin in Massachusetts started in October of 1986, when she turned forty and entered Masters competitions. Now, her timing was perfect. Massachusetts had races everywhere and many of them offered age-group awards and, for runners forty years of age and older, singled out those competing in the Masters age brackets (e.g. forty to forty-nine, fifty to fifty-nine, etc.).

For Robin, it was a wonderful opportunity to race without worrying any more about winning the outright female competition. There were many talented, younger women runners—a number of them famous nationally and even internationally—to take the top overall prizes, but Robin immediately established herself as one of the best female Masters runners in the state. She quickly learned just who some of her most formidable rivals were and, admits with a laugh, occasionally she was happy to learn what race one of them might be going to attend, so she could attend a different event.

As she told one journalist of this period in her life, "Running continues to mean a lot to me," said Emery in 1994, at age forty-seven. "I really enjoyed Masters competition. It is wonderful to see all the women competing today without having to go through all the social problems we did back in the 1960s."

In Maine, a number of her streaks of attending and running quality performances were coming to an end, especially at fall, winter, and spring races, starting, of course, with the Portland Boys Club and Bangor Labor Day 5-Milers. Robin and her new husband had agreed that she could return, alone, to Maine for the "three glorious months" of June, July, and August, living in her family home in Lamoine. A driven man, Joe Rappa worked on school matters and traveled to educational conferences throughout the summer. "He never learned to relax, never made time for recreation," Robin remembers, noting that Rappa tried taking up running for a short period of time in their relationship but it wasn't for him.

Returning to Maine meant going to all her favorite summer races. "One of my all-time favorites is the Great Cranberry Island 5K," the brainchild of the island brothers Larry and Gary Allen. She loved taking the ferry out to the island. She was charmed by the notion that the once four-mile race was now a 5K, shortened when the island itself was shortened in a tumultuous storm. And she loved the unique prizes, pieces of art or crafted useful items like the weathervane she received on one occasion; local artists made all the prizes.

She was free to return to Tour du Lac 10-Miler, Hancock 10-Miler, Hampden 8½-Miler, Northeast Harbor 5-Miler and Southwest Harbor 10K, and several Ellsworth-area annual races like the Grand Willey 10K and Union Trust 4½-Miler.

In Massachusetts, she discovered she was still running fast times and, in her new age-group classification, ranked quite high and was "starting to get known."

One of her greatest running career highlights came during the nearly fifteen-year Massachusetts period when she won the Masters division of the fifteenth annual Tufts 10K in October of 1991.

In a stellar field, the incomparable Lynn Jennings, from Newmarket, New Hampshire, had won in 32 minutes, 12 seconds, defeating the reigning Boston Marathon winner and world champion, Wanda Panfil of Poland. Jennings had won the inaugural event, called the Bonne Bell 10K, back in 1977.

This was Jennings's second fastest time on the course in nine appearances, earning her the $4,000 first-place prize for her third straight crown and fourth overall. She was a high-schooler the first time she won; she was also runner-up, four times, and placed third once. Jennings was a two-time World Cross Country Champion.

Robin, then forty-five, won the Masters title, in an outstanding time of 38 minutes, 03 seconds, taking forty-seventh place overall. The field had 3,785 female entrants (the all-time attendance record, set in 1983 when Joan Benoit won, was 8,453). Robin was identified, by the *Boston Herald*, as a resident of Bridgewater, Massachusetts, and winner of a $500 cash prize for her victory.

And, just one week later, in October of 1991, Robin took second place in the Masters women's division at the Harvard Health Downtown 5K in Providence, Rhode Island. She ran one minute and twenty-four seconds behind the winner, who ran 17:02, in another stellar forty to forty-nine division. The winner was Nancy Grayson of Columbia, South Carolina. Men's overall winner was Frank O'Mara of Ireland, beating stellar national luminaries like Doug Padilla and John Gregorek. Jennings won the overall women's title. Again Robin captured a cash prize; this time it was $600.

"I'd never won money before," Robin recalls, "It was really neat to get a check."

A very special career highlight came when Robin took tenth place in an elite Masters field in the World Cross Country Championships in Boston in March of 1992. It was a four-mile race conducted on a snowy golf course in Franklin Park. She remembers, "The young elites got to race on pavement; they made the old folks run round and round—two loops—in five inches of snow on the golf course. On the second loop, late in the race, I passed a rival who had been a national champion, someone I hadn't beaten before, to take tenth place."

In late November of 1992, Robin successfully competed in the Grand Circle National Masters, women's division, ages forty to sixty, 8K World Cross Country Championships. It was won in 31 minutes, 07 seconds, with Robin finishing fourth, in 32 minutes, 26 seconds. She was on the winning Liberty AC team, with combined score of 1 hour, 38 minutes, 17 seconds.

"I guess the best would be having two national championships at the 8K Cross Country Masters Championships in Boston. There was no money, but being a national champion is cool and they presented us with great medals," she says.

Robin enjoyed racing around Massachusetts, winning or placing well in Masters competitions. There was an extremely fast 5K course in Fall River, where world-class competitor Judi St. Hilaire won in a world record time (that was not ultimately allowed on a course technicality that the course was, basically, *all* downhill), but Robin ran a personal best 17-minute, 45-second 5K to win her Masters division and another cash prize.

On one St Patrick's Day she traveled into Boston's famed Irish community of South Boston and won the women's Masters division of a Saint Paddy's race. On several occasions she won her age-group division on Thanksgiving Day Turkey Trot events in eastern Massachusetts. Another event she thoroughly enjoyed was a race run along a footpath paralleling the Cape Cod Canal and yet another that involved running along a section of the dunes of Cape Cod.

Her new hometown newspaper, the *Attleboro Sun Chronicle*, carried brief accounts of some local events at which she scored well, often identifying her as the wife of the Attleboro school superintendent. In June of 1989, she won the Masters division of the Road to Good Health 10K, in a time of 39 minutes, 34 seconds (or six-minute, twenty-two-second

Robin wins women's title, Central Massachusetts Health Classic 5K, 1993.

pace), for eighty-second place overall, in a field of almost 500 runners. Stellar male performers Andy Ronan and Geoff Smith took the top two places, with Ronan winning in 30 minutes, 18 seconds.

In October of 1990, she won the women's overall division of the eighth annual Sturdy Memorial Health Chase 5-Mile Road Race. The newspaper reported that it was her second victory in a row at the race and her winning time was 31 minutes, 33 seconds.

Another local race that Robin outright won the women's division was the Attleboro YMCA 10K. In May of 1995, she posted a 39-minute, 53-second time and that was good for eleventh place overall in the race. The men's winner defeated his closest rival by almost two minutes and, the newspaper reported, "it was almost as big a blowout for Bridgewater's Robin Emery" who crossed with "no sight of another woman as the race winded down."

It was like old times in Maine as the newspaper interviewed her after this race. Identified as forty-eight years of age, she quipped, "I started to take off early because I am old and I wanted a good lead in case any young kids came later." The newspaper reported, "But the winner did not have to worry as the second-place finisher did not cross until 41:40."

And, once, at a small race in the community of Norfolk, where she was teaching school, she came as close as she ever would to outright winning a road race. "I was in the lead, and I covered the first couple of miles all by myself. I'd never been in the lead like this in a road race before. But then, I guess, a couple of men must have thought to themselves 'we can't have this' and overtook me." Robin took third place overall and was, of course, the first woman in the race.

By the year 2000, Robin and Joe Rappa agreed to an amicable divorce and Robin was free to return to her beloved Lamoine, and to teaching and running exclusively in Maine.

TEN

Robin's Fire Still Burns: Looking for Wrinkles, Gray Hair

IN 1967, WHEN ROBIN EMERY was twenty-one years old, it was almost as if she heard that Lamoine road calling out to her to run rather than walk for exercise. And two years later, she became a pioneer figure for females, appearing at races, after yearning for so long to have the kind of athletic career that males enjoyed all their lives, in school, at the local YMCA, and in community play, like Little League and Amateur Athletic Union (AAU) organized sports, etc.

At first, her inexperience in such competition made her so frightened she could barely tolerate her nerves. The good news was that she was pretty much the sole female present and, by running a low six-minute-per-mile pace, she earned deserved respect for her ability, finishing well up in the standings among her male rivals. When other young women began to appear, she was discovering that she not only loved the physical act of racing; she had talent for it.

By her late twenties, in the mid-1970s, she had already established her lifestyle and was well on her way to establishing a record that will be nearly impossible to equal. She was winning race after race after race, only rarely losing to Diane Fournier, the young Joan Benoit, and an occasional out-of-state competitor like Lynn Jennings. She was averaging winning between twenty-two and twenty-five races per year—and she would do this for nearly a decade!

Her new challenge wasn't nervousness over competing; it was fear of failure, with the newspapers and occasional television station either predicting another victory or reporting how "easy" it was for her to capture her victories and anticipating more completely dominating performances.

As she entered her thirties, she ran some of her best times, but found it hard to enjoy herself. The late 1970s and early 1980s brought a special popularity to her sport in American society. And the combination of the arrival of a number of young, talented female runners and regular media coverage of road racing left Robin with anxiety as she approached road races that were a weekly option, from the late spring, through the summer, and into the early fall.

Moving to Massachusetts as she was entering her forties, in the mid-1980s, was a wonderful happenstance for her racing career. The advent of age-group awards and the understanding by her sport that individuals in their later years deserved recognition for "winning" in their respective divisions meant that she no longer had to concern herself at all with winning the overall women's title. She was there to compete against any woman forty years old or older, in the Masters division. And because there were so many races all over eastern Massachusetts she could travel around, meet new people, and not worry at all about media expectations. In the early 1990s, Robin Emery had the opportunity to prove she was a national-caliber women's Masters division competitor, earning cash prizes and posting stellar times.

She actually enjoyed watching her anonymity slip away as she discovered the specific Masters rivals around traveling in that circuit and welcomed the opportunity to match paces with those individuals who were in her age division.

And runners, one must understand, are that strange breed of cat who actually anticipate and *enjoy* reaching milestone ages, like age thirty, age forty, age fifty, etc. Rather than dreading being a newly minted thirty-year-old, these runners can hardly wait to leave the naturally more-fleet decade of twenty- and twenty-plus-year-olds and take on some older rivals. It's a very normal conversation to have with a dedicated runner about when he or she is on the verge of entering a new age-group division and just how "excited" that individual is about the prospect.

Judith Blake, a Jackson Laboratory scientist specializing in genome sciences, first met Robin when she moved to Bar Harbor in the mid-1990s. She was in her forties when she moved to Maine and because the MDI Marathon was right in her backyard, she trained for and ran it: "And there was Robin. Robin immediately embraced my efforts. We cycle in and out of being in the same age group, so in and out of being competitive, but Robin was always finding me, asking how it was going. We've run lots of 5Ks, and many unique races around Down East Maine."

Blake says she can identify with some of Robin's pioneering spirit, running as a young girl: "When I was a teenager, growing up in the Connecticut countryside, I liked to run and my brother ran track. But there were no running options for girls. I would stop running if a car came down the road. Yes, the prevailing attitude was that 'girls shouldn't run.' Then I ran for fitness, two to three miles a day, during my twenties when I was mostly doing rock climbing and mountaineering. During the late 1970s, when I was living in Cambridge, Massachusetts, I would host Boston Marathon runners, but even though I was an active feminist, running Boston or any marathon was just not thought to be something 'girls' could do."

Concludes Blake, "I've very much enjoyed Robin's friendship and intensity. She has great stories about running and the changes in women's running over the years. And I know she led the fight in the early struggles to find support for women running."

Robin turned fifty years old in the fall of 1996. She was in Maine and ran running devotee and Penobscot County District Attorney Chris Almy's "Stop Domestic Violence Against Women" 10K in Almy's native home of Dover-Foxcroft as her celebratory first race as a fifty-year-old—and captured her first age-group title in the division.

Low six-minute pace for a race was, now, a memory. She was no longer concerning herself with time but the age-group rivals she faced. "Yes, being in my fifties wasn't such a bad deal but you start to notice your times aren't what they were. I could no longer do eighteen-minute 5Ks. My last nineteen-minute, sub-twenty-minute 5K came in Rhode Island, and now I was finding it weird to think a twenty-minute 5K is something awesome," she remembers.

She was then racing at a seven-minute-per-mile pace. "You feel like you're going as fast as ever. In the middle of the race, you feel like you're flying." And then that pace slipped back to eight-minute and nine-minute pace—and even slower.

Still, Robin finds the sport as much fun and rewarding as she ever has, in her fifties, then her sixties, and, now, just having entered her seventies.

"I just like running races; they give you that fitness test. I just want to continue to have that fun in my life," Robin states and cites an observation by Tom Derderian, well-known New England runner and author of the definitive history of the Boston Marathon. "He claims that when you reach your advanced years, you go to races for social reasons, to see everybody, meet with friends. He's kinda right."

But, lest you think her competitive fire is dimming, be assured—be *very* assured—it has not. The changing age-group divisions help restore that fire. Indeed, she only wishes it became a universal concept that age group divisions change every five years rather than every decade.

"It was a relief to get out of my fifties," she acknowledges with a laugh. She found, as she moved later into that age group, it was harder and harder to compete successfully with those newly entering the division. She believes it is much harder for those in the Masters categories to compete with rivals more than five years younger in the same division.

Robin doesn't see the need to break up the traditional twenty to twenty-nine and thirty to thirty-nine categories, but she argues that the Masters classifications should change to forty to forty-four, forty-five to forty-nine, fifty to fifty-four, fifty-five to fifty-nine, etc.

"I just don't think it is fair for a forty-nine-year-old to have to compete with a forty-one-year-old. We have people who want to keep going, who race just for racing's sake. Giving them five-year intervals gives them incentive," she argues.

Most races continue the early tradition of breaking up their awards in largely decade-long divisions. Yes, there is often an eighteen-and-under category and, at the other end of the spectrum a seventy-and-over division, largely established because races often do not have many participants in the Very Young and Very Old classifications.

She believes this so fervently that it led to a dispute with the individual who scored the annual race series for the central Maine Sub 5 Track Club. He quit doing the volunteer work because he found it both an unnecessary, additional time-consuming, record-keeping requirement and had concerns that race directors would have the burden of nearly doubling the expense of prizes to accommodate such a demand.

Challenged by the author of this book, who himself had a charity 5K race for twenty years, to raise money for local cancer research, that to ask sponsors to nearly double the expense for awards has got to be a concern, Robin responds, "Prizes don't have to be expensive—and this really isn't about awards as much as it is about recognition."

She cites her dear friend, the late Bill Pinkham, "People like Bill want to keep going. He knew his fastest days were well past him, but he raced just for racing's sake. He ran to place in his age division. But if we don't accept this idea then people are going to have 'no hope' for five years if we don't accommodate five-year intervals. We're old, yes, but we deserve recognition."

And she notes that at the race she and Tom Kirby created in Bill's memory, the Flat Top 5K in Lamoine, the prizes are little wood-carved buoys painted in Bill's favorite color and that, with some thoughtfulness, prizes can be meaningful and do not have to be expensive.

Her dear friend, Bill Pinkham, who served in the Maine House of Representatives for many years, was someone who shared Robin's passion for racing—for racing every possible weekend. They traveled together to races regularly for many years. In 2005, while competing at the popular 3K race in Bangor, on the Fourth of July, Bill ran his race and was in the downtown parking garage, out of the blistering hot sun, enjoying going over their respective races with a respected rival. Suddenly, Bill toppled over and could not be revived. An ambulance was summoned but he never regained consciousness. His death, later determined to be the result of a congenital heart condition unknown to him and his family, was a shock.

A skilled handyman, Bill had done a lot of work for Robin over the years at her home in Lamoine. "Like I said at his funeral, any time I go to the bathroom I think of Bill—but it's not what you think. Bill did

Another Labor Day race in the books!

so much work fixing my bathroom. He could fix anything." Robin poignantly charmed family and friends alike at a special memorial service for Bill, held in a packed auditorium of Ellsworth High School, when she began her remarks to the gathering, "Well, Bill, I hope you're happy—Here I am, in a dress!"

Almost immediately after Bill's death, Robin and Tom Kirby, another runner and friend, began discussing plans for a memorial race. Meeting with Bill's family, Lamoine town officials and so many other well-wishers quickly led to the formation of a race. Bill was known throughout the running community for his all-white, brush-cut or military-style "flat-top" haircut. Runners had playfully taken to calling him "Q-tip," for how easy it was to recognize him from a distance out on a racing course. Robin was very impressed and inspired by the participation of so many townspeople who wanted to help and be a part of the event, even though the sport of running wasn't important to them.

The event was set up as a 5K and Robin was thrilled when the very inaugural event drew 300 people. "I thought how great it was, with so many participating, running right past the cemetery where Bill is—and he could see them running past. It's so cool using the very roads I have been running since I first began running," Robin says. In late March of 2017, the Flat Top 5K celebrated its eleventh annual running, and it has become another important racing weekend that Robin adds to her continuing participation in the sport that means so much to her.

Judith Blake notes, "I have so much admiration for the effort she put into starting, and still running, the Flat Top 5K in Lamoine."

It was in the fall of 2006 when Robin turned sixty and, ironically enough, she found herself back at Almy's race in Dover-Foxcroft for that first race to be run as a sixty-year-old. She celebrated with a return to the age-group division winning circle by capturing a medal, so meaningful to her, she says, that it's an award she knows she's keeping.

Entering these new age-group divisions that are still decade-long propositions means for Robin that "everything is okay for five years—and then others come along to beat you. I see this as a situation where, essentially, I have at least five years on everyone else running. When I began running there were no other women running and so, if there are others in my age category it's very likely they started later than me and, probably, a lot later than me—and so they have younger legs because they did not run when they were younger. Today I have some rivals I regularly see, like Jeannie Butterfield; I now have three years running as a seventy-year-old before I'll have to face her in the same division again."

Still, Robin can see the other side of the coin and be quite bluntly realistic about the stage of life she has reached with the sport. "You know

I used to get quite angry when people called what I did 'jogging.' But now. . . . Well, maybe that's who I am now, a jogger. I do know this is a stage where you can't outrun dogs anymore."

Today, to do what she has always loved—and continues to love, she is willing to make concessions. Where she used to do sixty miles per week in training, she now does forty miles. She prefers shorter races and only does the occasional ten- or thirteen-miler.

Still the road warrior, Robin wins the seventy-and-over at 2016 MDI 13.1-Miler.

Michael Westphal, a 2016 Maine Running Hall of Fame inductee, was a consistent race winner in the late 1970s and early 1980s. He has recently earned national acclaim for courageously running with Parkinson's disease. Westphal says he has "been in awe" of Robin since they first met at a race through the woods in Lamoine back in 1973. He adds that she was "awesome then" and she's "even more so now."

Of course, many, many years ago she had decided to travel a far different path from the one many long-distance runners were obsessed by: the marathon. She says, "It's silly to keep doing marathons and training for marathons. You're hungry all the time. You're cold all the time. You're tired all the time. You're on the verge of getting sick and getting hurt all the time." So while others all around her (like the author of this book), were running one or two of them every year in the late 1970s and early 1980s, trying to lower a personal best or break a barrier—especially the sub-three-hour milestone—Robin had done four of them and written a fond farewell to the distance with never an inclination to reopen that chapter and that book ever again.

Where she has no interest in making concessions is frequency of racing. She goes to a race virtually every weekend there is one reasonably within traveling distance—and that is almost every weekend, starting in the spring, all through the summer and extending late into the fall. "I'm doing more races today than I did when I was in Massachusetts," she states. "I'm doing around forty-two races. There are even times I double-up, doing a race on Saturday and then one on Sunday. Mostly, I'm doing 5Ks. There are fewer and fewer of the longer races even available, like 10-milers or half marathons."

The races, she concedes, are what keep her going. "I don't seem to ever get enough of them. They're fun and they're what drives me to keep getting out there. I have been pretty lucky: I was born to run—and the goal, quite simply, is to be able to run tomorrow."

Her basic competitive nature doesn't seem to have lessened any either. At her last sub-twenty-minute 5K in Rhode Island, for instance, a woman attempting to keep pace with her tripped her, twice. After the event, Robin relates, "She came up to me and said, 'Oh, I'm sorry about my big feet.'" Still angered by the woman's irritating strategy to invade her

Ever the competitor, Robin enjoys what she calls "kicking wrinkled butt."

personal space to make herself competitive, Robin spat out caustically, "Yeah, well, that's *one way* to look at it."

Robin can even laugh at her own fervent desire to beat her age-group rivals or even avoid them. At the Cobscook simultaneously run 5K and 10K (both charitable events held for the benefit of a local hospice chapter), the challenging longer race concludes with a difficult final stretch on a hilly dirt road leading into a Cobscook Bay viewing area. Robin arrived one year to find a worthy, out-of-state opponent who sometimes summers in the area. She did a mock rant, for the benefit of the author of this book and some other friends, about "Who invited *her*?" and why the woman had to just show up, uninvited and unwelcome, to a race so consistently attended by regulars on the Maine road racing circuit. Since Robin isn't "above" finding out which race that rival is signed up—and jumping into the other event, I actually thought she was serious about the woman's "right" to show up and compete. "I was kidding," Robin laughs, recalling the incident, and explaining how the woman is, indeed, a regular summer resident of the area. She admitted that, yes, she has signed up for one race only to discover that that very rival has signed up for the same race; she returned to race organizers—and changed her participation to the other race where her chances to win her age-group division improved significantly.

No different than it was thirty and forty years ago, Robin is still concerned about just who her rivals might be when she attends a race. She remembers a recent race in Machias when she just obsessed about a woman who might be gaining on her, at any moment. "I killed myself to beat her. And, when I finished the race, I discovered that she was far, far back—nowhere near me," she laughs.

Going to a race and looking for your potential rivals is a little different proposition for her than it once was. "Today, I go looking for—wrinkles—and gray hair!"

So, yes, it still matters to Robin Emery to compete—and to win!

ELEVEN

Cabot Trail Relay: Twenty-Seven Straight Hours of Running Fun!

FROM 1998 UNTIL 2014, ROBIN EMERY and the author of this book were teammates who annually traveled to an event that billed itself as "the race of a lifetime." For once, gloriously, advertising does not overstate the product.

Indeed, for maybe, if there is that runners' version of *Field of Dreams*, a parallel universe to that magical baseball kingdom—where somehow time stands still and the running never stops—then the Cabot Trail Relay may be our little bit of heaven right here on earth.

The Cabot Trail Relay covers 276 kilometers, or 175 miles, a circuit that includes the Cape Breton Highlands National Park section of the beautiful, rugged northern terrain of Cape Breton, Nova Scotia. Using all of the historic Cabot Trail, it begins and ends in the community of Baddeck, once the home of the Scottish-born inventor Alexander Graham Bell, who loved the region for being so reminiscent of his native land. The relay is broken into seventeen individual races or legs, and each of the individual legs stretches between twelve and twenty kilometers (or seven to twelve and one-half miles). It is run for twenty-seven consecutive hours, starting at 7:00 a.m. Saturday and concluding by 10:00 a.m. Sunday.

Beautiful vistas are numerous and often spectacularly breathtaking.

On the eastern side, for instance, there is Leg 4, or Cape Smokey, the longest leg of the relay at twenty kilometers. On the climb up to its peak, the open ocean fans out seemingly forever, on the right. It features a tortuous, devilishly steep (at the very foot of it, a runner can actually lean forward, completely upright, and *touch* the incline!) 2.1-kilometer climb to that peak; memorable for the runner accepting this challenge are the numerous spectators who beat out a rhythmic pacing cadence on the vehicle guardrails in support of the gallant climbers.

In the early evening, the relay reaches the geographical top of Cape Breton and a gauntlet of three extraordinarily taxing tests: Leg 9, North Mountain, sets off with an uphill of 385 meters and then precipitously climbs 6.2-kilometers to its top (the race description bluntly states that this climb "makes Smokey look like a piece of cake"!). It is so treacherous, on all the mountainous legs, that vehicles accompanying the relay are not allowed to use any of the pull-outs en route to the top nor are team support members allowed to provide water for the team representative running; all vehicles must crest the summit and find level parking beyond.

Next comes Leg 10, MacKenzie Mountain: this features one of the area's signature portraits, pavement switchbacks, snaking back and forth, leading 6.2 kilometers to the top (an aerial portrait of this is available to tourists on everything from postcards to placemats, and a copy of the latter is presented free, at the awards banquet, to all participants on this leg).

Capping this mountainous *sundae* of running experiences is Leg 11, French Mountain. This leg is a largely straight downhill roller-coaster ride, run in blackness and reaching the western side of the island, where the runner can hear the ocean while measuring the onset of potential shin splints from the extraordinary experience of airborne strides followed by the inexorable pressure of feeling feet slamming into the front of running shoes, all while negotiating the return to sea level.

A final mountain comes on the so-called honor leg, Leg 17. This is the race's concluding section where one must negotiate the 3.5-kilometer climb up Hunter's Mountain before anticipating and then, finally, receiving the awe-inspiring welcome into downtown Baddeck as your team's anchor runner, crossing the last finish line of the twenty-seven-hour event.

The Cabot Trail Relay was first created in 1988 as a sort of United Way-like fund-raiser for the entire Cape Breton region, with proceeds from the event going to many community-based, nonprofit beneficiaries. The first year there were just six teams of seventeen runners, who "tested out the feasibility of the idea," in the words of the organizers. You bring in forty-five largely "from-away" teams with seventeen members, plus families, friends, etc., you get the entry fees, coupled with use of the local economy (hotels, restaurants, gas stations, gift shops, etc.) and you would provide a major boost to the region before the actual tourist season began. The trickiest element to be addressed, annually, is safety. From the very outset the relay organizers have worked closely with the Royal Canadian Mounted Police, and teams can be assessed time penalties for violating any safety rules while the runners and the relay's rolling cara-van of vehicles works its way around the route. Ultimately the relay has hosted as many as seventy teams at one time.

Starting precisely at 7:00 on a late May Saturday morning, the event then unfolds for those uninterrupted twenty-seven consecutive hours, finishing in downtown Baddeck, to an almost giddy-with-excitement crowd of tired runners, happy support families and friends, and a com-munity pulsing with vibrant energy. It isn't a traditional relay. There are specific starting times for each leg; any runners not able to reach the fin-ish line within a specified time allotment are simply assessed a five-min-ute penalty added to the time of the last runner to officially reach the finish line and be clocked by event timers. The specified time to match or beat works out to nine minutes, thirty seconds per mile.

Up until 1995, the teams were almost exclusively Canadian entries from the provinces of Nova Scotia, New Brunswick, Prince Edward Island, Quebec, and even Ontario. There were, however, one or two entries from communities in Massachusetts, with the town of Marshfield fielding a veteran team of runners that returned annually.

While visiting some relatives in Amherst, Nova Scotia, Dr. Peter Mil-lard, a two-time winner of the Sugarloaf Marathon and US Olympic marathon trials qualifier in 1980, saw a poster for the relay and imme-diately began putting a team together, registering his assembled friends for the 1995, or eighth annual, event under the name the "Maine-iacs."

When Millard invited the author of this book to be a member of the team, I remember vividly, being intimidated by the notion and concerned that I wasn't fast enough. My friend Peter went to great lengths to suggest that he was hoping to create a mixed team, men and women, of varying abilities, who might be good teammates and enjoy a very different kind of adventure with distance running.

That notion was blown all to hell when Peter, after all of us had completed the twelve-hour drive to reach Baddeck from Bangor by early Friday evening, returned from the relay's captains' meeting and announced quite simply to our little group, "I think we can *win* this."

Even for Peter Millard this was a particularly bold statement—considering we only had nine central Maine runners actually make the trip and now had to come up with individuals to run the other eight legs! In a particularly puzzling and amusing happenstance, a proposed local team of runners failed to meet the registration deadline. Organizers then were accepting only the first forty-five teams to register and, somehow, a basically Baddeck-area team had not registered in time and was left on the outside looking in. Peter had rounded up four of these men who agreed to run legs for our team; now, our four best runners—Rick Chalmers, Newell Lewey, Judson Esty-Kendall, and Peter himself—accepted a second leg to run. Team Maine-iacs could account for a runner to line up at all seventeen legs.

Now regarded as "such stuff as legends are made on," my inaugural run, on Leg 5, featured several amusing moments that were told and retold over the years—all at the expense of this book's author. A more than ten-mile leg, with many challenging upgrades, it featured a very long, steady uphill not far from the start. Support vehicles are not allowed to set off from the runners' start until, in waves, groups of them are released at ten-, fifteen- and twenty-minute intervals. I was already settled somewhere in the middle of the pack, working my way up this long, long uphill when Peter Millard pulled up alongside of me, in a van, with his wife adjacent to him in the front seat, and a number of my teammates in the seats behind him.

In my own defense, one must understand this: I was long past my prime, my absolute best days as a runner nearly a decade before. Now, having left the starting line, knowing the Maine-iacs team was already in—third place!—I was, quite frankly, miserable with the knowledge that God-only-knows where the team would be after I completed my leg.

So, did "Captain, my Captain" have any inspiring words for me?

Peter leaned out the driver's side window and, with a devilish grin, yelled, "C'mon, Ed, you've got to pick it up. You're *blowing it* for the whole team!"

I gave him the nastiest look I could summon while, at that very same moment, Peter's wife, Emily, leaned over and punched him in the arm, protesting the apparent savagery of the remark.

"Ed knows I'm kidding," Peter quickly responded to her.

Over the years when friends remind me of this exchange I continue to say the same thing: "Peter Millard is probably the only person who could have said such a thing to me" without getting a thoroughly vulgar response back.

On this very tough but very lovely stretch of road (it passed Ingonish Beach, entered Cape Breton Highlands National Park, and worked its way through the attractive little village of Ingonish), I was laboring after just a couple of miles and fighting to do anything better than a miserably pathetic eight-minute pace. I kept trying to petition an appearance from Ed-of-Better-Days-Past but it was definitely a losing proposition. It was a run that seemed to have no end. Finally, I saw a sign that told me I had 1K left to the finish. I marshalled my resources to give all I could to make the clock stop its inexorable tick-tick-ticking, adding more time to my team's overall time.

There was a turn off the main route, leading to a campground—and—there—was the finish line. And an ambulance just a few yards beyond it. I crossed the finish line and nearly lost my balance. I found myself being escorted right into the back of that ambulance, a medic on each side of me.

This led to—Indignity #1: A very concerned Judd Esty-Kendall joined us in the back of the ambulance. I was just starting to regain both my senses and my equilibrium. Judd eyed me nervously: "Ed, do you know who I am?" I snapped off both a caustic look and sarcastic retort: "Yesssss, you're—Judd." Relief washed across his face, replaced by mischievousness: "Good. Do you know who YOU are?!"

And this led to—Indignity #2: Suddenly, as Judd and I were both just about to laugh, Peter Millard, in a perfect swashbuckling entrance befitting this Theatre of the Absurd, leaped on to the back of the ambulance, shouting, "I'm a doctor—he's fine!"

The record shows that the Maine-iacs took third place in the 1995 Cabot Trail Relay.

And let the record also show that the four individuals we recruited from that aborted Baddeck-area team acquitted themselves nobly—especially the somewhat immortal (or at least mythical!) Fricker brothers, whom *NONE* of us ever met or even saw! Bert Fricker finished third overall on Leg 11 and brother Glen finished eighth overall on Leg 12—then off they went, we were told, back to their ocean workplace as fishermen! With the news of what a wonderful experience this was, the next three editions of the Maine-iacs had no issues filling up a complete roster, and the team finished second or third for the next three years. But around 1997 several of us felt that there just was too much pressure to perform, and we just couldn't enjoy the experience to its fullest. The team had a number of stellar runners, and if it were composed of seventeen outstanding runners it could surely compete for the top prize. Several of us stepped away.

Thus it was for the 1999 relay that Sub 5 Track Club president Fred Merriam began calling around with an idea he had. He wanted to put together a team of "senior" Masters runners (everyone would need to be fifty years old or older), male and female, and go up to the Cabot Trail Relay with the principal goal of having as much fun as we could with no concerns about how well we placed in the overall standings. Many of us, newly volunteering to join the proposed team, regularly competed against one another for age-group awards in races all over central, coastal, and northern Maine; now we would be teammates, encouraging one another and all running at a comparable pace. We adopted the name "the Maine Running Fossils."

And, of course, someone who embraced the concept from the moment she heard it proposed was Robin. "I'm someone who never got to be on teams, as a kid or in school. And running, of course, is usually such a solitary endeavor. I was excited to be on that very first team and, of course, that very first relay you go to is so amazing," she says.

The Maine Running Fossils had a group that included Fred and Joan Merriam, David and Katherine Wilson, Dick and Kay Storch, Robin Emery, Bill Pinkham, Ed Rice, Frank Woodard, Steve Norton, Rene Collins, Louisa Dunlap, Gene Ross, Dale Dickie, Gary Wakeland, Denny Beers, Anna Perna, and Earl Black—and many others over the years, from 1999 to 2014.

Within a couple of years' time Maine was sending four teams. First, of course, there was an elite team, "the Maine-iacs," featuring many of the best recent Maine college runners and outstanding members of the Maine road racing scene. There was an all-female team, with the playful moniker, "Maine Road Hags." A number of males who no longer could keep pace and find a place with Maine's elite team created a second team, "Team Rhino" (a nickname for founding member Kevin "Rhino" Dow), welcoming females as well. The members of all of these teams joked that, well, there was always the option of running for the Fossils when they got old enough—and no one else wanted them.

Most of the entries participating create that sense of "team" by designing racing singlets and warm-up jackets and leggings with their names. And then there are those teams that go for full-on costumes, spanning a range from honking geese and whiskered cats to gnomes to frilly silks and tutus! Any number of runners themselves have raced in complete costumes, to include Uncle Sam to men in drag. One guy enjoyed wearing a number of get-ups, annually: when he wasn't running he'd wear very provocative, naughty lady's attire on Saturday and, fittingly, for Sunday morning, a complete priest's attire.

With a touch that only a fashion guru like Coco Chanel could probably best appreciate, Robin stepped in to make sure the Fossils were properly "geared"-up for the event. She thought up, then designed, and ultimately took orders, had manufactured, and distributed any number of articles of apparel with our team name and various Fossil logos. She began with beautiful vests, with dinosaurs on the back, and our team name AND our individual first names on the front. She followed that up with berets that she, laughingly, credits all of us with "being good sports" to wear. There was the bright yellow windbreaker/rain slicker. And a baseball cap and a number of long-sleeved and short-sleeved jerseys for us to race in or just wear at the event identifying us as members of the Fossil team.

One year, tragically, we all wore buttons on those vests. It featured the always-smiling face of our captain, Fred Merriam, who had contracted a terminal cancerous brain tumor in late June of 2003 and died, one year later, in late June of 2004. David Wilson and I shared co-captaincy of the 2005 team. All of us ran the Cabot Trail Relay of 2005 touched by something Fred had said on his deathbed. And, in a brief statement to the organizers and all the teams gathered at the awards ceremony, David Wilson told everyone about the buttons and the heavy hearts with which we ran our individual legs. As we had prepared for our May 2004 trip to Cape Breton, the very stricken Merriam had wished us all well, saddened, of course, that he could no longer join us and would never be able to join us again, and left us with a poignant message. I know as I ran a night leg in 2005, crying frequently, I was grateful, very grateful, for both the solitude and the pervasive blackness.

At the awards ceremony to a hushed, massive assembly, David simply explained why we were wearing the buttons, how much Fred Merriam had loved the Cabot Trail Relay and closed with what Fred had told us about the 2005 event: "Well, next year, I'll be able to watch the whole thing."

As David walked back to our table, the entire assembled audience stood and loudly applauded, paying a final, wonderful tribute to our fallen captain, Fred Merriam. David, his wife, Katherine, and I shared a hug in the midst of our wonderful teammates as the thunderous ovation for Fred continued.

When our teammate and Robin's very dear friend, Bill Pinkham, collapsed and died just following Bangor's Fourth of July 3K in 2005, all the Fossils would have a second button to wear on their vests in 2006.

Still, trips to the Cabot Trail Relay became an overall joyous rite of spring for many of us, something we looked forward to all year long.

And the Maine-iacs, it should be stated with pride, have brought nothing but respect and honor to the state of Maine through the team's annual participation at the relay.

Joining original core members Rick Chalmers, Newell Lewey, and Judd Esty-Kendall have been such stellar road race veterans as Tim Wakeland, Jeremy Lisee, Evan Graves, and Judson Cake—and a continuing special congregation of "Young Guns," to include Adam Goode, Robby Gomez, Erik McCarthy, Ken Akiha, Dan Vassallo, Josh Zolla, Matt Homich, Jeff Ashby, Louie Lucchini, Knud Hermansen, Mike Bunker, etc. For many years Captain Brian Hubbell has led the talented team. One year, Gomez won his leg, shook hands with his closest rival as that young man finished—and then immediately went over to his Canadian girlfriend, who he had originally met at the relay, dropped to one knee, proposed, and delivered a little present he'd worn on his pinky finger on that victorious run—an engagement ring!

A number of years ago Maine-iacs member Ashby made a deal with the ownership of the Highwheeler Café, the popular downtown Baddeck breakfast and lunch/bakery establishment that members of all the relay teams came to love. The deal was that if the Maine-iacs won the relay five straight times the café would name a sandwich in its honor. The Maine-iacs had one stretch where the team won four straight times, only to narrowly lose to a worthy rival that fifth year; determined, the team subsequently returned and, from 2011 to 2015, did win five straight times, cinching an incredible record of achievement, posting nine victories in eleven years, plus creating a fun legacy, having a titled "Maine-iacs" sandwich prominently advertised in the café to be seen and purchased annually when the team returns to Baddeck.

In 2016, the Maine-iacs, having embarked on a new streak, set a new course record: 16 hours, 11 minutes, 38 seconds, breaking the Gray Hairs' record from 2010, of 16 hours, 16 minutes, 45 seconds—and won again in 2017. And the team members have a new food goal: they have an agreement with Tom's Pizza of Baddeck that, if they win five straight times again, the emporium will name a pizza in its honor—and the Maine-iacs can name the toppings a "Maine-iacs" pizza comprises!

In truth, only a handful of teams enter the relay with a goal of winning. Rivals like "Team Z," from Halifax, won that very first year in 1995, canvassing their area for a strong team and coming with a stated goal of setting a new course record for the relay—which they achieved, running it in 16 hours, 55 minutes, 28 seconds.

In recent years, the Maine-iacs have faced very worthy opponents, including the "Gray Hairs," comprised of mostly Windsor University (Ontario) alumni, the stellar outfit that defeated Maine in 2009, snapping the first streak to win the right to a "titled sandwich" and victors again in 2010; and a contingent of fast young flyers calling themselves the "Black Lungs," from Toronto, Ontario, who test the Maine-iacs each and every time they make the very long pilgrimage to Atlantic Canada.

There was one year where the overall feeling of community, shared fellowship, and fair play was briefly lost. With major sponsorship from a beverage company, a Canadian all-star team was put together, with Olympians and elite runners coming from all over the country for the express purpose of setting a new course record. The sponsor's signs and its product were everywhere participants turned. Yes, the team won, but failed in the effort to eclipse seventeen hours and lower the course record. The experience, understandably, left a very bad taste—pun intended—in everyone's mouth. The next year it was back to fair rivals and elite teams with representatives coming right from the area from which they were said to come, sans obnoxious sponsors.

Asked if she has any favorite memories from the Cabot Trail Relay, Robin surprised the author of this book by stating, "Well, yeah, that year YOU nearly died crossing the finish line on Smokey. I remember it coming over the loudspeaker: 'Will one of the Fossils please come help your runner?!' And I remember laughing when Fred [Merriam] said, 'Oh, he's all right.' Which, of course, you were."

Lest any reader think Robin, Fred, or any of my other teammates are showing less than appropriate concern for the health of a friend, it is important to note that, in my later years as a runner, I have suddenly developed this unpleasant habit of—ahh—dry heaving at finish lines when I have pushed myself to my limits. I'm almost as "on schedule" at doing this as Old Faithful is at Yellowstone.

It definitely happened the year I ran Cape Smokey.

And it would happen again the year when I was awarded the opportunity and ran the seventeenth and last leg to the final finish line of the relay.

Robin comes to the finish line, Leg 16, Cabot Trail Relay, 2002.

Several people took photos of my finish in the latter instance, including the unpleasantness that followed the finish, to the amusement or the shock of those unfamiliar with the routine watching it. Robin and her pal Bill "Q-tip" Pinkham put together a poster featuring an array of photos of Ed and his Leg 17 "fireworks display"; this was for an annual winter group run-and-potluck-feast gathering of friends at David and Katherine Wilson's home in Stockton Springs. It's hard to imagine that anything could be more side-splitting funny than Bill, in his droll, authentic Down East accent, doing a commentary as he personified the reactions of spectators showing, first, respect for my effort—and then ever-growing revulsion with the not-so-sanitary public "outburst" of mine. I think it may have been around this time that one of the Fossils (some are sure Joan Merriam said it) expressed the notion that "It's a good thing we have Ed—because if we didn't we'd have to make him up."

For one of these winter gatherings, Robin even developed an award, for "Dramatic and Near Death Finishes," to be presented to me for that particular year, and anyone else in future years who offered something comparable or memorable.

I'm just glad she wasn't around the year I was suffering and laboring to reach the finish line of Leg 16, one of the last times I would reach a finish line with an officially recorded time. I could see the race officials were just about to pick up the mat, thus stopping their recording device at the finish line, just before other officials set off the runners to start Leg 17. I thrashed and thrust my limbs in all directions to get myself to the line—and, mercifully, the officials left the finish line for me. As I walked back, I found Maine-iac star Erik McCarthy trying to catch a nap but clearly conscious for my finish. Slumped against a door of a car, he sleepily regarded me and then mischievously responded to my performance: "THAT . . . was Positively Operatic!"

Anyway, Robin didn't want to list any one specific personal memory, which shouldn't really surprise because, like the author of this book, Robin began running Cabot Trail many years past her prime. Asked if she sometimes wonders about how she might have done if she'd competed in her best racing years, Robin allows herself a moment to consider the possibilities. Wistfully, a glint in her eye and a quite confident smile accompanying her words, she replies, "I could have won a leg like Leg 3, probably in a record time."

Her good friend Judy Blake recalls how delighted she was when Robin invited her to join the Fossils and run the relay. "We would rent a car with one or two other Fossils and travel to Baddeck, figuring out how to make that all work with her teaching schedule and my work schedule. It's so much fun traveling with Robin because she is so excited about all runners, their efforts, their accomplishments. She enjoys sharing the competition."

Longtime Fossils member Denny Beers fondly remembers watching two of Robin's finishes, including the Maine Running Fossils' last appearance in the relay in 2014. The relay officials had moved on to start the next leg, but one of the relay's more compassionate teams, the Gnomes, had many of their members gathered in two lines, creating an honor lane of sorts to where the finish line had been.

Denny says, "The last two years that we ran, Robin did Leg 7, and both years the Gnomes brought Robin up the hill to the finish. They were chanting: 'Robin!—Robin!—Robin!' She had a big, warm, appreciative smile on her face all, the way to the finish." Denny adds, "I have always appreciated Robin's positive spirit, her 'Get out there and kick some wrinkled butt' attitude. No matter how long or hard a leg she had at Cabot, there was always that smile at the end."

In a far more serious vein, Robin and I disagree about the Maine Running Fossils no longer being granted admission into the Cabot Trail Relay because too many of the team's members can no longer officially make the cutoff times for the finish of each leg. We were warned, several times, that we were in jeopardy of no longer being accepted and, finally, in 2014, our application, after being accepted for seventeen straight years, was rejected.

We do agree that race organizers have every right to ban second-time entries from teams who are more inclined to party than to properly train and run. I've been disgusted by teams that arrive in Baddeck and their so-called runners can be seen walking, right from the starting line—or walking shortly thereafter, somewhere in the first mile.

What we disagree about is whether the race organizers should reject teams with multiple members who cannot do better than ten-minute-per-mile pace, or eleven- or twelve-minute. For me, this is posing an unnecessary burden of concern for a small but dedicated core of race officials, working twenty-seven straight hours to put on the best possible event they can.

For Robin, pure and simple, this is age discrimination. "If they want an elite race, they can have just five teams. What's the problem? Let anyone come, no matter how fast you are—let them in. They should make concessions for old people. Our older runners are doing the best they can—and they are unfairly being held to a standard that isn't reasonable."

She argues that teams with such runners already look out for one another and don't require officials or official timing to both enjoy the event and complete each leg. From the very earliest days of the relay, a five-minute penalty, added on to the time of the last runner to officially finish the leg, is assessed to any runner and team failing to meet that leg's standards. Nothing further is required from race officials, and she wishes the relay would reconsider.

For my part, I could not officially finish the legs I ran from the last three Cabot Trail Relays I attended. And I'm afraid I began feeling some shame about this; indeed, I found myself thinking, "You don't belong here anymore." I would have stopped—but I had one last goal to complete.

As I said, there are seventeen individual legs and pretty early on I was aware that the relay acknowledged those runners who completed the entire trail themselves over the course of time that their teams had participated. Every year I went up, I did a different leg. I didn't quite understand some of my teammates who kept wanting to run the same leg, repeatedly, either to improve upon an earlier time or because they just happened to really like that leg. I wanted a different leg every time.

Fortunately, for me, when the Fossils first began going to the relay, I opted for all the mountain legs, all the most difficult and challenging stretches. By the time I only had the shorter, more flat legs to negotiate I had already had a complete left hip replacement surgery and, shortly after my very last participation, I had surgery for a herniated disc that had been a bulging disc for many years.

In 2014, I ran Leg 3, the very last leg I needed. I collected the colorful plaque the race organizers give any individual runner who has completed the entire course on his or her own. I was prepared to waltz off into the sunset. But the Maine-iacs had one last beautiful surprise for me.

Every year the winning team receives, along with the individual awards, one of the uniquely designed Cabot Trail road signs, put up by the province's transportation department. That year, at the awards ceremony, the Maine-iacs asked me to come to their table—and they presented me with that road sign, in recognition of the feat of completing the entire trail.

And one year later, Robin Emery returned from her day of teaching school and found, on her porch, a Cabot Trail road sign. The victorious Maine-iacs had returned home and found a special way to pay tribute to her. "What a wonderful honor! I've put it in an upstairs window, facing right out on to the street. At night, whenever a passing headlight strikes it, it reflects and shines so beautifully. Yes, I've been fortunate to receive many awards and honors in my life. This is one of the very special ones."

TWELVE

Following in Robin's Special Footsteps: Sarah Mulcahy

OVER THE YEARS IT HAS BOTHERED the author of this book about some of those people, clearly very involved with the sport of running, who happily line up to collect the large number of prizes available at the end of an event. These can include individuals collecting the top prizes as the overall men's and women's finishers through the first, second, and third in a variety of age-group divisions, most frequently separated by only a decade, such as nineteen-and-under, twenty to twenty-nine, thirty to thirty-nine, etc. It's the ones who don't seem to know much about the history of the event itself or the special performers in that history or care.

Occasionally, a race director, like Ryan King at the Bangor Labor Day race, has even let me be part of awards ceremonies, just so I can gush about the history of the race. And, yes, gush about—Robin.

Yes, it bothers me, greatly, when people don't seem to have a clue about her extraordinary history. This is a very special history and people, especially, women, should know about it and respect it.

Sarah Mulcahy, fortunately, is someone who does.

The native of Eagle Lake and Aroostook County actually has a number of things in common with Robin, starting with the fact that she did not begin running until she was in college, around the spring of 2004. Of course, it had absolutely nothing to do with any stigma connected with the idea of females doing something completely unladylike. She recalls, "I always walked and enjoyed the time to be with myself while walking, but a friend of mine suggested I start running, and he was willing to help me get started. I decided to give it a shot and, in the beginning, I barely had the endurance to last a mile."

And, like Robin, the original connection had absolutely nothing to do with beating anyone or finding athletic glory; it was solely fitness based. "Once I got past that original struggle, however, I began to challenge myself to see how much farther or faster I could go. I ran just for my own personal health and fitness, and it became a hobby I looked forward to every day. It was my escape from everything I had going on in my life, for the hour or so I was out running."

Sarah did not start competing until 2009 when, on a whim, she decided to try two races in El Paso, Texas while out visiting her future husband, who was in the area for work-related reasons. One race was a 5K and the other an 8K. Sarah won her age-group in the 5K event and won first female in the 8K, taking second place overall.

"It was right then that I realized that I might have some talent for the sport, and I should do a little more research on proper training."

Clearly not easily intimidated, Sarah Mulcahy made her third-ever race Joan Benoit Samuelson's world-class-attracting Beach to Beacon 10K event in 2009. She remembers, "I cannot put into words how nervous I was to be running with some of the best runners in the world, but I quickly realized that the majority of people running were just like me; they were regular, everyday folks just trying to meet their own personal goals."

She continued running smaller races here and there, completing her first half marathon (the Maine Half Marathon in Portland) in 2011 and placing in her age group. She decided to train for her first marathon and made that the Sugarloaf Marathon in 2012.

She says, "I truly wanted to qualify for Boston, but had never run a marathon before, so I did not know what to expect." It ended up being eighty-five degrees, scorching hot, on race day. "Anybody who knows me knows that I do NOT race well in any temperature above sixty degrees," she says, surmising that condition owes to her Aroostook County roots. "I swear my body is just conditioned to cold temperatures. I prefer cool to cold race days with overcast skies." She ended up not qualifying for Boston that day, but "was determined not to give up."

Success came when she ran the Mount Desert Island Marathon in 2012 and qualified for Boston. She followed that up by running the difficult Bay of Fundy International Marathon in 2013, where she not only won the marathon but decreased her qualifying time for the 2014 Boston Marathon.

Sarah and her husband, a US customs officer, found out in November of 2013 that she was pregnant with their first child. Sarah recalls that she "consulted" with both her doctor and her husband and still ran the 2014 Boston Marathon. "I was six months pregnant, and I finished in a little over four hours, just enjoying the run."

Sarah states that she earned her first (and currently only) sub-three-hour marathon, running a 2:59:18, on that "grueling" Bay of Fundy marathon course in 2015, which is the course record. She ran the Fundy Marathon again in 2016, winning for the third time, but as it was way too hot for her liking on race day, she could not beat her own course record that day.

"I ran my entire pregnancy, including many smaller races, but now my daughter, Olivia, has a Boston Marathon medal in her room, as she has already run it without even knowing about it." She gave birth to that first child in July and ran the MDI Marathon in 2014 just a few months later. It resulted in a marathon personal best for her by twelve minutes! "Clearly," she notes, "less training and post-baby rest paid off. And 2015 was the year I ran some of my fastest times."

Sarah ran her fastest 10K time at the 2014 Beach to Beacon, in 38:11, earning a regional elite spot for 2015. To date, Sarah also holds the following records: Cobscook Bay 10K in Pembroke, in 2016, with a time of 39:07; the Flat Top 5K in Lamoine in 2015, with a time of 18:47. The latter is the race Robin Emery created to celebrate the life of her late running friend, Bill Pinkham.

She found out she was pregnant with her second child at the beginning of August 2016, a week or so after she had run the Beach to Beacon that year. She ran throughout her second pregnancy, until late January of 2017, when a fall resulted in a fracture of her hip by the ball of her right femur at thirty-one weeks pregnant. Surgery, requiring a plate and two screws, has brought her hip back to "normal," but "I am now out of

Sarah wins 2015 Bay of Fundy Marathon.

the running scene until further notice. I am hoping to return in a few months, but it could be about a year."

Sarah Mulcahy believes that she and Robin first met back in 2012 at the Labor Day 5-Mile Road Race in Bangor. She had become a member of Sub 5 Track Club at the end of 2012, after running her first Cobscook Bay 10K race in June of 2012. She had moved to Washington County at the end of June in 2011, so the 2012 Cobscook Bay 10K was her first race in Washington County.

At the Labor Day race, she learned about the Sub 5 Track Club with its race series and points accumulation process. And, she recalls, "I learned all about Robin from other members of the club, especially at the Labor Day Road Race. We instantly connected once we met, not only because of our love for running, but also because of our connection to education. When we get together we always talk about our jobs and careers in education."

Sarah is a middle school math and science teacher at the Woodland School. Her fastest Bangor Labor Day Race was in 2015, finishing in a time of 30:29, noting that she has not equaled or surpassed Robin's fastest time at the race.

Sarah recalls, "I began to learn about Robin's history at the 2012 Labor Day Road Race, because [race director] Ryan King always explains the Robin Emery Award and her contribution to running when presenting the awards."

Of Robin, Sarah, says, "The more I learned about Robin and how pivotal she was to the women's running community in Maine, the more I respected her and appreciated her friendship. I've always asked her for advice and listened to her suggestions about how to become a stronger runner. She is someone I will always look up to."

She states, "I won my first Labor Day 5-Mile Road Race in 2013 and could not have been more honored to receive the Robin Emery Award directly from Robin herself. She truly is an inspiration to me, as well as many other female runners in the state of Maine. Her perseverance to succeed and participate in a sport that was male dominated when she started proves to all runners, both male and female, that runners can accomplish their dreams if they are willing to work hard and not give up."

She continues, "Regardless of the conditions, Robin is out on the roads, and I am very much the same way. It doesn't matter how far you go or how fast, just get out there. Receiving the Robin Emery Award at the Bangor Labor Day 5-Mile Road Race three times has been so very rewarding to me. Robin exemplifies the spirit of running, and I could not be more honored to have received the award in her name, especially since she presented it to me with a gigantic hug and fantastic smile."

Sarah credits Robin further, noting, "If I had to compare myself to Robin's personal history with running, one saying comes to mind and it's one I use in my classroom daily: 'Never Give Up.' Any time I would tell Robin about a race I was running, she'd challenge me to 'go for the record' and if it was her record, she'd say, 'Go beat my record. You can do it.'"

She adds, "Robin always has a positive attitude and always helped me to see the good when I was struggling due to injury. She encourages me to keep going and know that these are only minor setbacks."

Sarah Mulcahy concludes, "Robin and running go hand in hand and this leads me to the bigger lessons I have learned from Robin. If you have dreams, chase them. If you have goals, set yourself on the right track to meet them. Nothing is going to be given to you. Success is the result of hard work, perseverance, and determination. I still have a dream of one day meeting the qualifying standard for the Olympic trials in the marathon distance. Although I am unsure if I will be able to due to the most recent hip fracture, I will continue to set goals for myself and push myself to achieve these goals. I hope to be a role model for my children that they can do anything in the world they want to, as long as they are willing to work for it."

THIRTEEN

Robin's Future Goal:
To Be a Fast Ninety-Year-Old

BECAUSE SHE AVERAGED SOMEWHERE between twenty-two and twenty-five victories over the course of her first fifteen years (1972–1986) of racing the Maine roads, Robin Emery has won, at a minimum, 255 overall women's titles in an incredible career. At the time of her induction into the Maine Running Hall of Fame in 1992, in just the hall's second induction class, this statistic was included, and it seems impossible, nearly incomprehensible, that anyone, male or female, will come anywhere near matching this feat for winning foot races.

Fortunately, Robin no longer feels the need to "apologize" for posting her earliest wins as the sole female in the race, noting that those low-six-minute-per-mile-pace miles were "pretty good." Indeed, when other women began joining this true women's pioneer runner, they had plenty of opportunities to beat her—and they could not. Over the course of that *first decade* of racing in Maine, she lost less than a dozen times.

Of course, there is that absolutely spectacular record at Maine's two oldest, most revered races: she won the Portland Boys Club 5-Miler an unequaled nine times, with a personal best of 29:06 in 1981. She won the Bangor Labor Day 5-Miler an incredible fifteen times, with a best of 30:01. In 1998, just a month shy of her fifty-second birthday, she won the race and captured the trophy named in her honor!

In a 2015 article for the *Ellsworth American*, Taylor Vortherms quoted the then-fifty-seven-year-old Joan Benoit Samuelson as paying tribute to

Robin this way: "It was Robin who set the bar really high for me. She and Diane [Fournier] were the two leaders in Maine." And the Olympic gold medal winner added, "I will always have great respect for Robin's leadership and passion. I'll never forget Robin and Diane's contributions to the sport." Neither should anyone else in Maine.

Robin Emery has come a long way—literally and figuratively—from that young woman running alone, in a hoodie and baggy pants to hide the fact that she was a woman, running in graveyards and at night so people wouldn't see her, so that people wouldn't make fun of her or threaten her.

Today, she thinks, "I don't know what we were afraid of. It was just different then. You felt weird. Now I look back and wonder what was the big deal?"

In a 1984 *Bar Harbor Times* article, entitled "Robin Emery Is Hooked On 'Healthy Addiction,'" Robin recalled, "A few men were running but women weren't supposed to do that stuff. Even my parents thought I was crazy. But I guess they figured it was better than drugs."

Of course, her dad grew to become so supportive that he regularly attended her races and photographed her. And her mom too, who died in 1993, learned to become supportive: "She began to realize I'm not stopping—so she might as well go with the flow."

The "flow," with regards to her reading, film, and music interests has changed little, but her passion for them remains great. She has always loved history, majoring in the Pre-Columbian era in college and maintaining a love for historical fiction, polar exploration, and mountaineering. She is, she states quite proudly, "what you would call a Civil War buff. There is a certain feeling I get about that time in history that is hard to explain, but I like to go through the battlefields and 'hear the echoes' of that time. I have read extensively on the war years. I also am extremely interested in Pre-Columbian America and early Colonial history." That leads quite comfortably into a love of films that range from old Westerns and historical depictions. "I especially liked *Band of Brothers*; it made me feel closer to my dad's generation, seeing them as young men. *Chariots of Fire* is my favorite film about running. I think they got the tone of that age very well." For the former flute player, her musical ear leads her to be quite at home with Beethoven, Handel, Mozart, and Haydn, but she can just as easily crank the volume on Rock 'n' Roll favorites like Queen, Kiss, and Boston or press play for country, bluegrass, R&B, and Celtic selections too.

Being the truly unique person she is, Robin has always moved to the beat of a drum she wants exclusively in her own hands. She is, after all, the woman who has always loved cars, moving from a hot, late-1960s vintage Mustang, through a succession of colorful VW Beetles, then on to Subarus, Mazdas, and Saabs, to a decked-out, four-wheel-drive Escape and, now, her beloved Jeep Liberty.

Then there is the woman who has always loved motorcycles too and is proud owner of a 250 Honda Rebel, a gray street bike she has nicknamed "The Gray Ghost" or, simply, "Mosby" (her love of history and the American Civil War leading her to name it after the Confederate general or his moniker). She uses the motorcycle for trips to and from the golf course, enjoying the gas savings but principally enjoying—you guessed it—the speed. She calls riding her bike "the closest you can come to flying on the ground that there is."

And then there is the woman who found what she had determined, finally, was the perfect Nike model running shoes for her. No, she didn't just buy one or two back-up pairs. She bought twelve pairs of them, storing the spares for her inevitable future use. Oh, and then came the clothes. Robin is pretty sure any prize money she won went directly into her racing and training gear. To start with no clothing designed specifically for women and then find herself with nylon stuff, Gore-Tex stuff, "tech" (lightweight, moisture resistant) stuff, tights, and on and on, meant buying such clothes is what she terms her "one vice."

Having the stability of her education career meant she had a job she has always found rewarding and the months of June, July, and August to devote entirely to her passion for racing.

Having taught for nearly fifty years, she says, "I became a teacher so that I could make a difference, however small, in someone's life. I had some pretty awful teachers growing up and it influences your self-esteem and confidence. I wanted to help students find their strengths and realize their potentials, and increase their self-confidence. I have taught for nearly as long as I have been running and when my former students come back and say they went into history because of my class, it makes me feel fulfilled."

She taught the fifth grade for all those years, with no special support instructors. "We had to teach music," she says, with a shrug of her shoulders. "We had thirty kids in our class; now they have eighteen." It's been her professional life for almost fifty years; now, finishing up her career back where it first started, in Ellsworth, she works as what is known as an "ed tech," or special teaching assistant to the classroom teachers. "I actually like this better than a specific classroom assignment because I get to work one on one with the kids and get to move around to working with all the grades."

For thirty-seven years, Jim Newett has had a pretty special observation deck for watching Robin. Today, the principal for the Ellsworth Elementary Middle School, since 1989, notes, "Robin Emery was a name I quickly learned when I started teaching in Ellsworth in January of 1981. Robin taught grade five and I taught grade six across the hall. It wasn't education that we largely talked about, it was running. Thirty-seven years later we are still working together and the topic of conversation continues to be about running."

Newett continues, "I'll now ask, 'Where did you race this weekend?' Robin will then go on to tell me about her latest conquest on the road, and she'll ask how I'm doing. All I'm thinking about is how incredible it is that Robin is still running and still winning her age group (she was *so* excited to turn seventy!). She doesn't miss a day of training. When I tell her I take a day off a week, I can almost see her cringe at the prospect of her ever missing a day. That's Robin. She totally loves the sport. It gives each day meaning, the race experiences put her to the test, and the pre- and postrace socialization connects her with friends she holds dear. It's been that way a long, long time and it's a beautiful thing to see," says a man who has run and completed twenty-four Boston Marathons, with a streak of twenty-two consecutive ones that continues to this very day.

A two-time winner of the Bangor Labor Day 5-Mile Race himself, Newett has some special memories: "While Robin's longevity is truly amazing, I had the privilege of sharing my short-lived 'glory days' with

Robin during her reign as the top woman runner in Maine, which spanned decades. We both won the Bangor Labor Day race in 1984 and 1985, and it was very special to have two teachers from the same school on the TV sports news on the same night and to see our pictures in the *Bangor Daily News* the next morning. Throughout all of Robin's triumphs, she has been gracious, humble, approachable, and friendly. That's Robin, too."

Newett adds, "While we now take for granted the presence of women runners at road races, Robin lived through the times when that wasn't true. Training, let alone racing, was forbidden for females, but that didn't stop Robin. She would disguise herself in bulky clothes and run. She would hear the lewd comments out of car windows and run. Items would be thrown at her and she would still run."

Jim Newett concludes, "Robin followed her passion despite the obstacles, and doing so was critical in breaking down the barriers in a male-dominated sport. Robin wasn't a banner-waving zealot, she was a young lady who simply wanted to run, and her example paved the way for the many ladies who have followed her lead. Robin truly is a 'pioneer' of women's running, and, to me, that is her legacy. The seeds she planted have spread far and wide, and women runners now have equal footing with men on the running scene. Her example, her fortitude, her passion, and simply her love of running has been with her for her entire career that started well over fifty years ago and continues to this day."

Ever the educator, in playful but pretty honest mode for the George Stevens Academy students, in the John Wiggins 1983 *Ellsworth American* piece, Robin had these tips for the beginning runner: "don't blow your nose into the wind in a new training suit; don't assume a car will get out of your way because a 3,000-pound car will win in every encounter; wear reflectors; don't make noises like a deer in hunting season; 'nice doggie' won't work; and you and a car will hit the big puddle at the same time."

Obviously, Robin Emery has never worried about any long-term harm she might be doing to herself, running or racing. In talks, like the one she gave at George Stevens Academy in 1983, writer Wiggins quoted her as mocking any of the unrealistic positive outcomes right on through to the outright devastating prognostications from medical experts. She said these ranged from "great," because running will "cure depression," to "frightening," citing a New York cardiologist who claimed that running "can kill you." This doctor, Robin had playfully tried to draw the students into seeing as a complete quack, said the sport would both "turn your joints to jelly" and "will cause female organs to get unstuck."

Then, at age thirty-seven in 1983, Robin told the students that she had run over 25,000 miles in the last eighteen years, equal to one trip around the world. She was then averaging 3,600 miles per year.

At that talk, Wiggins recounted, Robin asked the students to take their pulse beats for ten seconds and multiply the count by six. Most, she said, would have a pulse rate in the seventies. "Some marathoners have a pulse rate of thirty-eight. Running gives you a lower pulse. I figure that your heart has only so many beats ahead of it, so why use them up all at once."

Her heart rate might have been the only concern her running might have meant to her overall health. She has weathered innumerable injuries, handling them as just a part of the landscape of being a great athlete: You compete, you get hurt, and as soon as your body tells you it's repaired, you return to compete again.

In the early days, there were stress fractures and heel spurs. She knew the flimsiness and thinness of her running footwear, especially in the heel, contributed greatly to this problem. Like her friend, Dick Goodie, she tried to rectify the situation by cutting up little pieces of carpet and inserting them into the shoes to buttress the support. This wasn't a very successful solution, and she "limped around a lot." It wasn't until she met the popular and well-known podiatrist, the late Dr. Roy Corbin, and was outfitted for orthotics that she, finally, found the proper solution. She had Achilles problems. Sometimes she'd do something entirely unconnected to training and competing, something "stupid, like trying to move a refrigerator at school" and she'd have sciatic nerve problems.

Over the years, the worst moments, it seemed, tended to be those runs when you'd have to walk most of the way back home, sometimes in the dead of winter. In 1999, she suffered one horrendous skiing accident, when someone on a mountain bike plowed into her, breaking ribs and her collarbone; in the incident she "could feel the muscles all tearing off the shoulder blade." That injury was particularly weird because her shoulder was in a cast but her legs were fine; of course, she could not run. But every single time, with every single injury, she'd just start on the road to recovery, lifting weights when she could or walking, as soon as she could—so that soon after that she could start running again.

It would never occur to her that the lifestyle of being a runner isn't worth risking injury, no matter how great. As she told students at George Stevens Academy in that 1983 *Ellsworth American* article, "we runners feel better at work and play. We have the lifespan of a Galapagos turtle, and we are more confident. After you run a marathon, you feel differently about yourself. You have done one of the hardest things in the world. You get 'the invincible syndrome.'"

Says noted runner, noted educator and coach, and fellow Maine Running Hall of Fame member Danny Paul, who first saw Robin when he was a schoolboy competing at the Portland Boys Club race, "All I can say about Robin is she is one of my heroes. In the world of Maine roads she was so amazing and so warm at once. I always felt honored when she acknowledged me as a fellow runner."

Outstanding runner and longtime Cobscook Bay 10K runner Jonathan Aretakis states, "Robin is such a peach. The Cobscook Bay 10K would be only half the race without Robin. She's told me it's one of her favorite races. As a race director, this is so gratifying to hear!"

Of course, today, Robin enjoys competition just as much as she ever did.

Shortly, after turning seventy years old, in the fall of 2016, Robin did the annual Pet Run in Old Town, a popular 5K she's run for many, many years. "I felt great—and I now have the course record for a woman seventy years old and older." She ran 31:07, which, she notes wryly, included "dodging dogs at the start." It is gratifying to her that there were three other seventy-year-olds in the race, and that she broke her friend Mary Alice Bruce's earlier record. She believes that, shortly, races will begin to have to create a division for eighty-year-olds.

She frequently talks about running into her eighties and her nineties. "Why not?" she says today. "I am going to keep running no matter what. You see people in their eighties and nineties still running. My new plan over the past few years is kicking wrinkled butt," adding that there is no

Robin celebrates her fiftieth year on the roads by winning the seventy-and-over age division at the Black Bear 10K in May of 2017.

special place anywhere that she needs to go, happy to run races in Maine for as long as she can.

She saw her future, speaking to the youngsters at the school in Blue Hill in 1983, and she's still following the same blueprint. The *Ellsworth American* quoted her as saying, "Running has become as much a part of me as sleeping and eating. I am into it for life, and I want to be a really fast ninety-year-old. I am addicted, body and soul. I like myself better when I run. I can't stop."

FOURTEEN

Road Racing in Maine: Running in the Footsteps of Those Who Loved the Sport as Much as We Do

ROAD RACING IS A SPORT WHERE YOU can feel all alone, running in the company of roughly 36,000 strangers at a major marathon—and a sport where you can feel the presence of so many friends, respected racing rivals, and training buddies, living and dead, while running alone, warmed by your memories.

Running. It's as basic, as simple, as it gets: You just put one foot in front of the other. And repeat.

You need so very little to run. Economics play no factor. Never, ever have. A jersey, a pair of shorts, socks and a pair of running shoes (yes, for some of us, a stopwatch is almost more essential than all of the above BUT the shoes).

Also optional, but essential for many of us: a dream.

Even someone who is the epitome of the Mediocre Athlete can start with so little and become so much more. That's exactly what the author of this book learned firsthand through personal experience—and used to tell about myself to young people with whom I worked as student-athletes in my two years as a high school cross-country coach. Especially the ones walking around wearing the name-and-number jersey of some famous athlete.

Joan Benoit Samuelson, winning women's division of Benjamin's 10K, 1982

"You know who my favorite athlete is?" I'd ask those of whom I was quite sure knew me well enough that they would guess a famed Red Sox player, like Ted Williams, or famed Celtics players, like Bill Russell or John Havlicek, all of whom I nearly idolized as a boy.

And I'd smile—and I'd say, "No. The answer is—me. I spend my time, every day, thinking about my training and my goals, and pursuing both.

And that's what I would wish most—for you. Become YOUR own favorite athlete. Invest—in yourself."

It's true that as a young boy I could never, ever imagine myself as the hero of my own sports fantasies. I'd be Bill Sharman or Sam Jones, sinking the winning basket for the Celtics—or Jim Piersall or Gary Geiger, making the key defense play to save the day for the Red Sox. Never, ever could "Eddie Rice" imagine himself finding personal athletic satisfaction.

Even running a 5-minute, 11-second 1-mile, in Army fatigue pants and combat boots at Army basic training on a track at Fort Dix, New Jersey, in the summer of 1971 or regularly proving to be the first of the forty-eight-member Charlie Company to cross the two-mile finish line did not do anything for my athletic self-esteem. When I was lapping fellow company members on the track, flying along, alone and far outdistancing the others, I remember thinking to myself, "So, *THIS* is what it feels like to be—Kenny Flanders!"

Almost a decade later, owing to the extraordinary support of so many in the Maine running community, and training daily under the caring guidance of Steve "Silver Fox" Norton, I began to find my running "voice" and went on to enjoy a career of nearly one-quarter of a century where running became a passion so vital, I could quite honestly repeat the mantra of a friend of mine: it was my religion; it was my mistress.

And for people like Robin Emery and me, running means we are part of a running continuum, a glorious living history.

There are some members of our generation who only cheat themselves, I feel, by believing we somehow "invented" the true sport of running, with all the innovations in equipment and shoe design technology, in training techniques, in diet- and health-related information to incorporate, and the advent of so many annual races encompassing the entire calendar year, with age-group awards, celebrating far, far more than just overall event winners.

Some, sadly, think of our running "forefathers," people like Clarence DeMar (still the all-time champion of the Boston Marathon, with seven victories, the first coming in 1911 and the last in 1930), Johnny Kelley (who won two Boston marathons, in 1935 and 1945 and completed sixty-one Bostons), and Maine's own Penobscot Indian Andrew Sockalexis (second in the Boston Marathon, in both 1912 and 1913, and fourth in the marathon at the 1912 Olympic Games) as slow, plodders—as guys who were just fortunate to run before running became popular.

To dismiss them, so inappropriately, is to dismiss a wonderful history.

You see, I still get chills running anywhere along Route 2, from Old Town to Bangor and up to the old racetrack at the Bass Park complex. To run anywhere along that route is to run, literally, in the footsteps of DeMar and Sockalexis, who once dueled in an eight-member field for a nineteen-miler on Sept. 21, 1912. DeMar had traveled by train, accompanied by a small group of racers from his North Dorchester Amateur Athletic running club, from the Boston area, to capture a victory over his newly discovered great rival from Maine, who finished second that day.

These earlier runners ran a highly laudable, by any runner from any era, five-minute pace, in drab running kits and flimsy shoes, having largely worked long, hard, manual jobs all week. They used the trains to get to the Boston Marathon or the odd race here and there in the East. There were very few races anywhere to be found, and only the top three finishers generally were rewarded for their efforts, receiving a silver cup or useful prizes like shaving kits and sweaters.

Hardly glamorous and not the least bit glorious, these amateur men truly ran for the love of the game. Amateur status was prized and safeguarded closely; the nearly despised, so-called money-chasers actually found very few opportunities to run for cash rewards. The professional ranks were reserved for match races (two runners of great reputation pitted solely against each other) and fairgrounds team duels (matching a pair of Caucasian runners versus black or Native American runners), both hopeful of attracting a large gambling pool to properly reward both the winning competitors and the race promoters.

Ultimately, I think anyone who looks closely at the history comes to have a great respect for anyone who ran in these early years—and, perhaps, comes to the conclusion I came to: a great runner would be a great runner, in any era.

So, while my generation may not have "invented" running, we did have an admirable "run" beginning in the mid-1960s, gaining full momentum through a "running boom" in the 1970s, a glory period in the 1980s, and a popularity that carries through to the present day.

Shortly after Dick Goodie's fine book, *The Maine Quality of Running*, was published in 1984, I hoped to publish a companion tome, selecting ten outstanding men (Bruce Bickford, Ken Flanders, O. J. Logue, Carlton Mendell, Peter Millard, Andy Palmer, Danny Paul, Hank Pfeifle, Andrew Sockalexis, Ralph Thomas) and five outstanding women (Joan Benoit Samuelson, Robin Emery, Diane Fournier, Kim Moody, Carol Weeks) to be the focus of more in-depth profiles. Unfortunately, no Maine publishing house was interested.

Today, as I look back at the names I selected, I recognize that they epitomized not only what a special runner looks like, but what special individuals each one of them is as well. Benoit Samuelson, of course, has written her own autobiography, and the author of this book has written a biography of Sockalexis. And in my earlier pages, I looked at Maine's pioneer female runners, Robin Emery, in detail for an incredible career spanning fifty years—and still counting!—and Diane Fournier, in one detailed, special tribute, chapter. The other eleven individuals, too, I believe are no less worthy of having their stories told and here, briefly and in alphabetical order, I would like to pay special tribute to each of them (relying principally on information for their "*The Runners*" credits from each one's biography on the website for the Maine Running Hall of Fame):

Benjamin's 10K, 1982

BRUCE BICKFORD

The Runner: Bickford won the state high school two-mile championship twice outdoors and once indoors, and took first place in the mile twice indoors and once outdoors. After placing third as a junior, he won the New England Cross Country Championship meet in his senior year. That 1974 race, Bickford maintains, is still one of the most rewarding wins of his stellar career. At Northeastern University, he twice earned All-America honors in track and cross-country. In his senior year he won the Greater Boston Collegiate Cross Country Championship, the indoor IC4A two-mile title, and the New England steeplechase championship. He qualified for the Olympic trials in three events: the 3,000-meter steeplechase (8:27), 5,000 meters (13:30), and 10,000 meters. Bickford deserves to be remembered for his impressive 27:37.7 clocking in a track meet at Stockholm, Sweden, on July 2, 1985. It turned out to be the fastest 10K run that year in the world, and it gave him a No. 1 ranking by *Track and Field News*. In that race he beat the 1984 gold medalist Alberto Cova, as well as the world 10K record-holder, Fernando Mamede. He once held the American record for three miles until it was beaten by Alberto Salazar, and over his running career he qualified for seven US national teams. His career bests include: mile, 4:01.8; two miles, 8:30.6; three miles, 13:06.7(American record); 5K, 13:30 (third fastest ever by an American); 3,000 meter steeplechase, 8:25.3; 10K, 27:37; 15K, 44:43; ten miles, 49:29; 13.1 miles, 1:06.32; and marathon, 2:18:57 (Boston, 1987).

The Man: Bruce, largely known as "Bick," grew up on a farm in East Benton, Maine, the oldest of three boys, all of whom became runners. Bick's father, Stanley, asked his boys that they limit their extracurricular time at school to two sports. There were plenty of chores that needed doing on the farm and there was not time for more "play" than that. It was while Bick was trying to do some milking before school one early morning during his senior year of high school that he got frustrated and punched an uncooperative cow, breaking his hand. And that is how he came to win the New England Cross Country Championship, easily, running with a cast on one hand and wrist! One of his all-time favorite memories is returning from that race, alone with his coach, to be greeted at a huge surprise party in the gym of what appeared to be an empty school on the weekend. He raced internationally, to get better, rather than stay in the United States where he could have run road races for money and prizes. Bick endured the heartbreak of earning the alternate's role, for both the 5K and the 10K, with fourth-place finishes at the US Trials in 1984. He returned to those trials four years later, punching his ticket for the 1988 Olympic Games in Seoul, Korea, on a rainy track in Indianapolis, running late into the night as officials had waited and waited for a break in the weather. A Boston newspaper, fittingly, wrote a headline over the photo of Bick winning: "Sometimes nice guys finish— first!" Once, Bick told the author of this book, he set all his personal bests in races he didn't win. "How can you be upset about that? You have to enjoy the moment when you've done your best."

KEN FLANDERS

The Runner: One of Maine's most celebrated high school runners, the Deering High of Portland ace won the following: State Outdoor two-mile, 9:45, 1968; 1968 Maine State Cross Country Champion; State Indoor one-mile, 4:23, 1969; State Outdoor one-mile, 4:25, 1969; 1969 Maine State Cross Country Champion; State Indoor one-mile, 4:22, 1970; and State Outdoor two-mile, 9:25, 1970. Flanders went to Northeastern University and, by 1973, he had been crowned New England collegiate champion in both the two-mile and six-mile. And through this decade he would race to seven victories in his favorite event, the Portland Boys Club 5-Mile Race. In 1972, Flanders won the New England 6-Mile in 28:45, then went on to take sixth in the NCAAs, a race won by Steve Prefontaine. In 1973, at the New England Indoor Track and Field Championships, he ran a personal best two-mile, winning in 8:50 while defeating talented Dan Moynahan of Tufts. One of three best career races was a seven-miler he ran while attending Northeastern. With Bill Rodgers in the field, Flanders led for the first four miles before Rodgers came along to win it. Flanders's best career times include one mile, 4:12; three miles, 13:55; nine miles, 45:12; and ten miles, 50:33. He was named Maine Runner of the Year in 1980. "He should go down in Maine running history as one of Maine's top five distance runners. He had ability at all distances, from an 8:47 two-mile to a sub-30:00 10K on the track," says educator and coach Brian Gillespie.

The Man: Ken's father, who struggled with alcohol abuse, died when Ken was eight years old; his mother worked forty or more hours a week her whole life, paying all the bills and keeping their home immaculate. There wasn't much extra money, but she always made sure Ken had Converse basketball sneakers and running shoes so he could participate in school sports. They didn't own a car, so he was lucky to have some older runners take an interest in his running talent, and they would drive him to road races during his mid-teens. His mother would always give him a few dollars for food and to help with the gas for these trips. With his moustache, his long, flowing hair, and his beautiful long-legged racing gait, Kenny Flanders seemed liked the personification of the rock 'n' rol-

Portland Boys Club 5-Miler, early 1970s

lin' 1960s, blazing away in a pair of running shoes. He was brash, and he backed up predictions of course records and victories with matching actions. He was the acknowledged "chairman of the board" of the Maine Rowdies, racing elites who ran fast and partied hard. Once he and some Rowdies pals arrived for the start of a race in a limousine that pulled right up to the starting line and allowed them to make a grand entrance and take their places in the front row. Their parties were legendary—but no one ever broke the code of talking about them. The Rowdies did an annual charity, 400-mile relay run of the entire state for the benefit of Pineland mental health facility. "I like to run up front and control the race," he once said. At one rural race, a director found himself tongue-tied trying to explain how one country road tied into another on the race route. "Just follow Flanders," he said, stating the obvious for many races in Maine during his era of dominance.

O. J. LOGUE

The Runner: By the time he had graduated from Orono High School, Owen Joseph Logue had starred on three state championship track teams. In 1973 he took fourth place in the state two-mile championship, and in 1974 he was second in the state 1000-yard competition. He won the two-mile event at the Penobscot Valley Conference Championships and then took fourth in the event at the state outdoor championships. In his sophomore year at the University of Southern Maine, in 1977, he took fourth place in the NAIA regional qualifying meet in cross-country. The year 1981 was a very memorable one for him when he posted the following times: Boston Marathon, first Maine finisher, 2:26:06; Maine Coast Marathon, first Maine finisher, 2:27:44; Kingfield 10K, 31:47;

World Deaf Olympics X-C race, 1981

Tour du Lac 10-Miler, 52:47; Bar Harbor Half Marathon, 1:11:37. Also in 1981, Logue became the first Maine Deaf Olympian, representing the United States in track and field at the Deaf Olympics in Cologne, West Germany. At the US trials he finished in the top three in three different events—5K, 10K, and 25K. At the Games in Cologne, Logue set personal records for himself with a 15:01 clocking in the 5K, good enough for seventh place, and 31:36 in the 10K, for sixth place. He also took sixth place in the 25K. Logue would qualify for the Deaf Olympics of 1985, held in Los Angeles, but had to drop out of the marathon due to injury. He made his third US team, for the New Zealand games in 1989, but did not compete because of a family illness.

The Man: From the moment he drew his first breath, O. J. Logue found health challenges that most individuals would surely have found nearly insurmountable and most definitely outright prohibiting where athletics were concerned. Yet he overcame deafness, speech impairments, and severe asthma to establish the mental and physical determination to achieve success through running. After earning his BA, O. J. earned his master's degree in education from the University of Maine at Orono in 1981 and later his doctorate in education from Vanderbilt University in 1992. He has served as the Associate Dean of Academic Services for the College of Education and Human Development at the University of Maine and has served on countless local, state, and federal boards, councils, and commissions all related to bettering the lives of people with special needs. Recently, he has accepted the post of executive director of the Maine Educational Center for Deaf and Hard of Hearing in Portland. He has also coached both cross-country and track athletes, at Bangor and Orono high schools, and at the University of Maine. O. J will always prefer to talk about his involvement in charitable endeavors rather than any personal success he might have enjoyed. There was the Rowdies annual 400-mile relay, which he ran five times. And in 1982, O. J. did a thirty-mile solo benefit run that raised over $9,000 for the family of Adam Hodge, an eight-year-old battling leukemia. It was during this run that O. J. met the love of his life, Barbara, a fellow runner and, today, lifelong supporter of his running endeavors. "Running for charitable events was always more satisfying than running for myself," O. J. says.

CARLTON MENDELL

The Runner: Mendell was a nationally ranked veteran road racer who made a name for himself as an ironman, running marathons and ultra-marathons. Running his very first road race at age fifty, Mendell had run one hundred marathons by age seventy-three. In 1992, at age seventy, he ran the second-fastest marathon in his age group in the country, 3:30 and, when he was seventy-one, he set North American records at 100K and fifty miles. Mendell first got involved in distance running in 1971 after reading an article about Portlander Dick Goodie and ran his first road race in the 1972 Portland Boys Club 5-Miler. He quickly became an avid runner and a prolific road racer, running sixty to seventy races a year that typically included six marathons, three in the spring and three in the fall. By age sixty-two, Mendell, who was six feet and 144 pounds, had set

Casco Bay Marathon, late 1970s

fifteen national age-group records. In February 1993, at age seventy-one, he set North American age-group records for 100K (11:27:10), and fifty miles (9:21:53). In September of 1984, at age sixty-two, he finished first overall in a twenty-four-hour race at Brunswick, Maine, covering 125.5 miles. When he was sixty-four, he won another twenty-four-hour race at Westport, New York, in July of 1986, covering a distance of 100.5 miles. In 1992, he ran a total of eighty-four races, and by the time he was seventy-nine, he'd run 135 marathons. He was named Maine Track Club's Runner of the Year in 1989 and was chosen Maine Runner of the Year in 1992. He was *Mainely Running* magazine's "athlete of the month" twice. He was also presented with the Bruce Ellis Award by the Central Maine Striders in 1987.

The Man: A native of New Bedford, Massachusetts, born in 1921, Carlton credited his involvement in athletics to an aunt who gave him a membership at the New Bedford YMCA. He went to Western Maryland College on a football scholarship. He also ran the 880 in track and took second in a meet against Johns Hopkins in 1941. He did some racing after college as an aviation cadet at Monroe, Louisiana, where he ran the half-mile. In 1940, he played semi-pro football for the Murphy Club of New Bedford, Massachusetts, and in 1947, he played in the New England Pro Football League with Lonsdale in Rhode Island. He was lead navigator of a B-17 when the Eighth Air Force bombed Berlin in 1945. In the greater Portland area, he made his living as an insurance agent and, by his own admission, he lost a good many years to alcoholism and ill-effects from divorce. By the late 1960s, he stopped drinking and then he stopped smoking. Irritated by seeing his weight increase to 220 pounds, he determined he must start exercising and then he discovered running in an article about fellow veteran Goodie. So one day in 1971 he went down to Baxter Boulevard. "I ran to one telephone pole—sixty-five yards—and I walked to the next," he told *Maine Sunday Telegram* columnist Sara Hobson in 1987. "It took me two or three months before I could do a half-mile." And from this humble start, the affable gentleman, known to attend races in formal attire, dress shirt, tie, jacket and slacks, ran distances at times for his age-groups unlikely ever to be matched or surpassed. He died in 2012.

Winning the Sugarloaf Marathon, 1984

PETER MILLARD

The Runner: Despite the hot conditions at the 1980 Boston Marathon, Millard managed to run 2:21:55—good for thirtieth place overall—and this wonderful effort secured a place in the US Olympic trials later that year. What was exceptional about Millard's performances was that they came at a time when he was training to be a doctor. Millard and his training partner, Kurt Lauenstein (later a multiple-time winner of Portland's Casco Bay Marathon), deprived of quality training time by a work schedule that could stretch to a hundred hours or more a week, used to snatch time between patients to sprint up and down the stairs of the hospital building; on other occasions they would run their interval sessions around the parking lot so that they could—in the days before pagers—be on call for emergencies. At Cheverus High School, Millard was a 4:20 miler before there were many 4:20 milers: state champion, 1000 yards; Southwestern Maine champion, 880 yards and mile; co-captain, state champion cross-country team, 1972. At Amherst College, he set the freshman record for the mile. While at Amherst, Millard became interested in the marathon and ran his first Boston Marathon in 1975, a 2:34 effort from the twenty-one-year-old Millard. He ran 2:28 in 1978, 2:25 in 1979, 2:21:55 in 1980, and 2:21:21 in 1983 at Philadelphia. Millard won the Sugarloaf Marathon (1983 and 1984), the Philadelphia Boathouse Marathon (1989), and the Elks Club Midi-marathon in 1:07:34 (1979).

The Man: No, in all honesty there is not a great "body of work," as a racer of roads, but what there is, is truly of an elite caliber; Peter put his professional career as a doctor and public service above racing goals. It began when Peter hitch-hiked from Maine to Bolivia and back after graduating from college, volunteering in an Indian hospital in Cochabamba before starting medical school (this adventure undertaken solely to determine whether he wanted to become a doctor); later, Millard would decline a general anesthetic when surgery was performed on his knee—so that he could study what the surgeon was doing. At the age of thirty, when many marathoners are approaching their peak, Millard made a decision that effectively ended his career as a national-caliber athlete. He accepted a posting to the Willis Pierce Hospital in Mt. Selinda, Zimbabwe, as a staff physician—one of a handful of doctors responsible for looking after nearly half a million local inhabitants. Indeed, in Mozambique there are 0.04 doctors per 1000 population, one of the lowest in the world (That's four hundred doctors for ten million people). He and his wife, Emily, worked for three years in a rural hospital in the mid-1980s, during a time of war just across the border in Mozambique, and, in his words, "it was an intense experience of human suffering and survival." After returning to the United States, he earned a PhD in public health and did clinical work in HIV/AIDS in North Carolina. After returning to Maine, he worked for the Centers for Disease Control's Epidemic Intelligence Service and, later, served as a faculty member in the Bangor Family Medicine residency for thirteen years. He returned to Africa in 2008, to Beira, Mozambique, where he worked for five years, teaching in a medical school and running the teaching clinic. It was there that Peter developed a new minimally invasive technique for male circumcision to prevent HIV. "I don't personally have a patent or get any money, but it is definitely my idea and I've done all the research to prove it works. The scientist must be separate from the development and commercial aspects," he explains.

KIM MOODY

The Runner: Moody, a native of Gorham, competed during the 1970s and 1980s and became one of the best marathoners and ultra-marathoners in the nation. She was a national champion at fifty miles, running the second-fastest time ever by an American and the third-fastest in the world. She also placed seventh in the 1985 Boston Marathon, one of only three Maine Running Hall of Fame members to ever finish in the Top 10 at Boston, recording her personal best of 2:46. In 1981, she ran the Maine Rowdy Ultimate 24-Hour competition on the campus of Bowdoin College, finishing first among women. Moody later ran many ultras, including the Rowdy 50-Miler in Brunswick, which she won several times. Of her ten career marathons, she won both the Casco Bay Marathon and the Maine Coast Marathon several times each. In 1983, she finished first among women in the Chicago National Championship 50-Miler, in a time of 6 hours, 30 minutes. Moody was named Maine's "Runner of the Year" three times—1979, 1980, and 1982. In 1984, at Lake Waramaug, Connecticut, she ran the second-fastest time ever run by an American at fifty miles, recording a time of 6:01. It was just a minute off the American best and five minutes off the world best. She even ran the prestigious and grueling Western States 100 several times, taking third place in 1984 in 20 hours, 55 minutes. Her time of 2:51 at Boston in 1984 qualified her for the US Olympic Trials Marathon; she competed in the trials that year as well as in 1988.

The Woman: As a young girl, Kim dreamed of being a dancer and loved all kinds of dance, from ballet to jazz to contemporary. She would ultimately capture the lead singing and dancing role in a local community theater musical production where the author of this book, then the theater critic for the *Portland Press Herald*, gave her a glowing review many years before he would ever come to know her and become a friend. Unfortunately for the entertainment world, the dancer's body evolved more into an athlete's body; the transformation came the year she spent as a high school foreign exchange student in Norway, cross-country skiing to and from school. A 1981 University of Southern Maine graduate, Kim earned her master's in Primary Care Nursing and adult nurse practitioner license at Boston University, in 1984. She earned her PhD

Winning the Maine Coast Marathon, 1984

in Nursing Science from the University of Washington–Seattle in 1994. Her research and publications have come in the areas of HIV, chronic disease care, and substance abuse prevention. She has been a professor of nursing at the University of Southern Maine for twenty-five years and has served for thirty-five years as a clinical nurse in critical care nursing; she currently continues as a nurse clinician in the cardiac intensive care unit at the Maine Medical Center in Portland. Kim developed a community collaboration with the Portland Community Policing Program and worked with nursing students to mentor youths and families in the Parkside neighborhood of Portland dealing with serious drug issues. The program helped to increase school attendance, decrease substance use, and strengthen family-school relationships.

ANDY PALMER

The Runner: He was a runner who strove for and achieved "a lifetime of fitness," but for someone who did not begin running until he was twenty-three years old, his rise to nationally ranked status was, indeed, meteoric. By the fall of 1977, he was competing against Maine's very best runners and took fourth place in two straight Aroostook County races. He won a race held in Fort Kent, the first of many wins. Following this, Palmer soon realized that he had endurance and moved up to the

Northeast Harbor 5-Miler, late 1980s

marathon, winning a race in the Maritime Provinces. He then decided to move to Boston in order to run with the very best in the world. In Boston, in the late 1970s, he trained with Bill Rodgers, Greg Meyer, and Kevin Ryan. Things really began to fall into place for Palmer in 1984, and he became a nationally ranked runner. At the prestigious Cherry Blossom 10-Mile Road Race, Palmer ran 47 minutes, 52 seconds, a finish good enough to be ranked tenth-fastest American for the distance. In 1984, he also ran for an American record at the 30K distance for twenty-nine-year-olds. He qualified for and ran in the Olympic Trials Marathon in 1984 and 1988, and was thirteenth in the trials for the World Championship Marathon in 1986. Among his other times were: 3:55, 1500 meter run; 4:13, one mile; 29:04, 10K; 2 hours, 16 minutes, marathon.

The Man: Andy pursued an education related to physical and mental health and attained the following degrees: BS in Health, Physical Education, and Recreation, University of Maine at Presque Isle; MEd Physical Education and Administration, Springfield College; MEd Exceptionality, University of Southern Maine; PhD Educational Psychology, Florida State University. For most of Andy's professional career, he was a teacher and mentor. In 1995, after attaining his PhD, he developed a private performance enhancement practice. His focus was on helping aspiring runners to develop the mental and emotional skills to succeed. He also believed strongly in the concept of pursuing "a lifetime of fitness," something he was heard to say many times. He directed and owned the Maine Running Camp at Bar Harbor, beginning in1980; was head coach at Craftsbury, Vermont, from 1988 through 1995; and, in 1995, became a sport psychology consultant for Roy Benson's Nike Running Camps. Andy and his wife, Zika, established a fitness center, called ZAP Fitness, in Lenoir, North Carolina. This facility housed around thirty runners and hosted fitness and performance seminars. The purpose of this facility was to provide a high level of support to emerging athletes, with the proceeds from the camps, seminars, and workshops going toward supporting six to ten post-collegiate distance runners. Andy's training philosophy was based upon the principles of periodization in training and patience in attaining results. Tragically, Andy died of a heart attack at age forty-eight, while on a training run in 2002.

DANNY PAUL

The Runner: From 1969 to 1972 he ran on five state championship teams (two in cross-country, one in indoor track, and two in outdoor track). He ran a 4:28 mile and 9:23 two-mile at Portland High. Paul attended Northeastern University from 1972 to 1976 and recorded times of 4:17 in the mile, 9:07 in the two-mile, 9:02 in the steeplechase, and 29:31 for six miles on the oval. He was also runner-up in New England's steeplechase and was Greater Boston champion in the steeplechase in 1974. Paul says that his three best lifetime performances were his 24:20 5-mile at Franklin Park, Boston; a 30:16 10K; and a 1:07:52 half marathon. During the 1970s, 1980s, and 1990s, he won major half marathons in Maine, including the Elks Club event in 1977, the Cape Challenge in 1989, and the Maine Half Marathon in 1993, the last at age thirty-nine. He was named Maine Runner of the Year in 1985. From June 1979 through July 1995, Paul won a total of fifty-eight road races. On two occasions he won two races in one day. As a Masters runner, Paul finished eighth in the National Masters 8K in Boston in November 1994. His best career times include 4:17, mile (1975); 14:48, 5K (1975); 24:20, five-mile (1979); 30:06, 10K (1983, 1985); 51:54, ten-mile (1977); 1:07:16, half marathon (1974); 2:24:58 marathon (Ottawa, 1984); 9:02 steeplechase.

The Man: As a boy, Danny came to deeply resent a father who abandoned his family; years later, when Danny was preparing to enter college that father contacted him and offered to pay for his education. Danny remembers defiantly rejecting the offer, telling him, "You've never cared or concerned yourself about me before; I can do fine without you now." He would need an athletic scholarship to attend Northeastern University and for his first three years he needed to fend off all contenders to replace him. One coach even marveled, "Well, they've come every year to take your place—and you're still here." Unfortunately, in his final year, Danny lost his athletic scholarship and had to complete his education at the University of Maine at Farmington. There, however, he would meet his future wife, Tammy. Danny is as great a coach as he is a runner. He has been named Maine High School Coach of the Year eight times over the years in cross-country and track. From 1977 through 1993 he coached twenty-two state championship teams in

Old Orchard Beach 5-Miler, early 1970s

track and cross-country; his winning record in girls' cross-country at Greely High from 1983 to 1993 was 194-0 and included five state titles. At Falmouth High, Danny's boys' cross-country teams have captured four state championships and his boys' outdoor track teams have won four state championships; his girls' outdoor track team has won one state championship. Danny has likewise achieved great heights as an educator. An English teacher, he was recognized by the Walt Disney Corporation as one of thirty-six outstanding teacher/coaches across the nation in 1994. Popular singer/songwriter Jackson Browne was a special guest at the event and Danny remembers feeling especially honored when Browne wanted to meet him, that one teacher who "teaches Shakespeare and runs Boston Marathons."

HANK PFEIFLE

The Runner: For sheer speed and depth, the period from the late 1970s until the mid-1980s was a golden age of Maine road racing. In an era when winning times for local 10Ks were routinely under 31:00, Pfeifle scored three Maine Runner of the Year awards, in 1981, 1982, and 1983. Pfeifle in fact ran some brilliant races against the likes of Bruce Bickford, Bill Rodgers, and Andy Palmer, beating each at various times in his career. The races were, perhaps, never widely appreciated in Maine; they took place in venues outside the state. He has been thought "an athletic work in progress" from his days as a skier and runner at the University of Vermont through his road racing career and finally as a bike racer. As for his most memorable race, he picks the 1980 Boston Marathon (twenty-first in 2:20:34) for achieving some clear goals and in the way the race unfolded. The last four miles saw Hank move from thirty-fifth

Besting Bruce Bickford, out of state, early 1980s

to twenty-first and achieve an Olympic Trials qualifying time. He also lists the 1976 USTAFF Championships, where he ran "a solid race" in star-studded company and the 1978 Maple Leaf Half Marathon, winning against a national field in a fast time. His personal bests include 3K (indoors)—8:03, BU Invitational 1983; 5K (indoors)—14:05, BU Invitational 1984; 8K—22:53, Sub 4 8K Championship 1983; 10K—28:46 Natural Lite 10K 1981; 15K—45:32, Tulsa 15K 1985; ten miles—48:42 New Jersey ten-mile 1982; 20K—1:00:41 New Haven 20K 1982; half marathon—1:04:37 Philadelphia 1982; 30K—1:35.34, Albany 1981; marathon—2:16.27, Houston-Tenneco 1985.

The Man: After graduation from the University of Vermont, Hank and wife, Beth, eventually moved to Dallas, where he ended up participating in Ken Cooper's 1975 legendary study on American distance runners, featuring other subjects such as Frank Shorter and Steve Prefontaine. Later, upon hearing that Hank ran 60:41 for 20K at New Haven, a then national record for a thirty-one-year-old, the exercise physiologist exclaimed, "That's impossible: he doesn't have the values!" In his forties, Pfeifle deemphasized his running career and began to race bicycles. He upgraded to a Category 1 racer at age forty-eight. It was a predictable level of achievement for an athlete who is tough, talented, and committed to be the best at whatever he tackles. He has some outstanding national and international credits as a Masters cyclist. They include 1998, World Masters Games, first, road race division (age group forty-five to forty-nine) and third, in hill climb; 1999, USA Cycling upgrade to Category 1 (highest racing grade for amateurs); 2001, USA Cycling Masters Championships, third, road race (fifty to fifty-four); 2007, Tour of Sardinia (seven-day stage race in Italy), two stage wins (fifty-plus); 2012, USA Cycling Masters Championships, first, road race (60-64); 2013, USA Cycling Masters Championships, second, time trial (sixty to sixty-four); and 2016, USA Cycling Masters Championships, first, road race (sixty-five to sixty-nine). Balance has been a critical ingredient in Hank's life, and it is encouraged by his wife, Beth, who jokingly says of the Maine running years that "I was lucky enough to own my own race horse." The racing was incorporated into family life with Beth taking her racing turns and their children joining in as well from time to time.

RALPH THOMAS

The Runner: The muscular, barrel-chested, five-foot-six, 145-pound Penobscot Nation native was legendary in his own era, dominating the roads throughout New England in the 1970s and early 1980s. He followed in the footsteps of 1912 Olympian Andrew Sockalexis and his own brother, Jack, who had been a state champion in both cross-country and track. Ralph ran during his freshman and sophomore years in high school but then quit. It would be years later, at age thirty-three, that he would be encouraged to take up running again by his minister. Over the course of his career Thomas ran more than a dozen sub-2:30 marathons. His best was 2:23:30 for forty-fourth place at Boston in 1975 when he was thirty-nine years old. It was one of two American age-group records he set in the marathon. His other national record was 2:27:21, run when

Winning the Monmouth 15K, 1978

he was thirty-seven. He was the oldest man to qualify for the 1976 Olympic marathon trials at age forty. Thomas was ranked by *Runner's World* magazine as the sixth best marathoner in the country in 1975. His lifetime bests included 24:40 for five miles; 31:17 for 10K, 1:06:39 for the half marathon, and 2:23:30 for the marathon. He was inducted into the Maine Sports Hall of Fame in 1990.

The Man: Ralph had every right to grow up filled with anger and resentment. As a young boy, a teacher pulled the one Indian lad in her classroom into a boys' restroom and rubbed his nose in urine for which another student had been responsible. He battled alcoholism and seemed, for a time, to live for his next barroom fight; one time, his wife recalled, the target was so much larger than he that Ralph had to get a running start to jump up and take his next swing. He did hard, physical work for a living, typically fourteen hours a day, as the last of the state's independent poultry contractors. He and his crew worked through the night, picking up chickens, putting them into crates, loading them on to trucks, and hauling them off for processing. Fitting in training to run was never easy. And races were rarely close by. On some weekends, when he'd ventured out of state, he'd run a race on Saturday, sleep overnight in his car, and run in another race on Sunday. He'd then return home and work all night with his crew. Like America's earliest runners, Ralph was right out of the working class. Not a man with a lot of money, he could not afford to have two pairs of running shoes. He trained and raced in the same pair. And of course, he wasn't into fancy running outfits. He raced in his usual black nylon shorts, still stained with salt from his last workout, and he usually wore his tattered sleeveless T-shirt with holes in it that he probably wore to work, too. This was the Ralph Thomas runners loved. They couldn't picture him any other way, and this is partly what made him the living legend he was.

CAROL WEEKS

The Runner: She became one of Maine's best female marathoners, winning the Paul Bunyan Marathon three years in a row from 1979 to 1981. Her best marathon time of 3:01 was run in 1981 at Casco Bay. Weeks joined the Run to Win Ladies Team, coached by Brian Gillespie. She became one of the team's best runners and was able to improve her 10K time by over two minutes to 39:56. As a member of this team, Weeks was part of one of the best Masters teams in New England. In 1992, they won the Sonesta Women's 5K State Championship and were third in the National Masters 8K Women's Cross Country Championship in 1992, 1993, and 1994. They won the Maine State TAC 5K Women's Championship in 1993. In 1994, they won the New England Masters 5K Series Championship and the Maine Women's 5K Distance Festival Championship. In the New England Championship Series, Weeks finished second overall through individual scoring of three races. Her PRs include 5K—19:27; five miles—31:45; 10K—39:56; ten miles—66:05; half marathon—1:29. She was a member of the Winnipesaukee Relay Masters record-setting team. She has also been Runner of the Year for both the Central Maine Striders and the Maine Track Club. A few of

Winning the Paul Bunyan Marathon, 1980

her more recent running accomplishments include the following: Beach-2Beacon 10K, August, 2016, first in age group sixty-five to sixty-nine, 50:03; Falmouth, Mass 7-Miler, August, 2016, third in age group sixty-five to sixty-nine, 57:29; Great Island 5K, October, 2016, second in age group sixty to sixty-nine, 24:10; Great Pumpkin 10K October, 2016, second in age group sixty to sixty-nine, 49:21.

The Woman: For almost forty years Carol was an educator, an excellent one who found the career "extremely rewarding." She began as a teacher in 1975 and retired from work in the education field in July of 2014. Over the years she has worked in seven different school systems in Maine and held a variety of positions including teacher, guidance counselor, assistant principal, principal, and assistant superintendent. Her focus, she says, "was always on providing the best possible education for students. I feel so fortunate to have had a career that I enjoyed so much. I took a special interest in helping students who experienced a variety of problems and struggles." One such student was a deeply troubled young girl with a very bad home situation. She had been a stellar high school performer. At the time Carol was working as a guidance counselor at the Mahoney Middle School in South Portland. The girl had already shown great talent and her coach, Brian Gillespie, thought that developing a relationship with Carol might help with the total person. He was exactly right. The young girl was living and working in South Portland and "we developed a strong friendship which has continued through the years. We stay in touch these days through Facebook," Carol notes, of the young woman who continues her winning ways racing on the roads of Maine. In addition to her racing, Weeks has contributed to the Maine running community in other ways. She was co-president of the Maine Track Club in 1992. She also co-directed the Peaks Island Road Race. Carol has served on the Board of Directors of the Maine Running Hall of Fame and the Maine Track Club.

These runners are, of course, just a small sampling of the very special talent that was found in this era racing all around the state. Start thinking great runners and you can just start ticking them off, to include Bob Hillgrove, Dave Farley, Larry Greer, Sammy Pelletier, Michael Gaige, Gerry

Dick Goodie and Robin Emery, training together, early 1970s

Clapper, Bruce Ellis, Anne-Marie Davee, Bob Winn, Bruce Freme, Steve Podgajny, Marjorie Podgajny, Red Dean, Bernd Heinrich, Chris Snow Reaser, Michael Westphal, Sheri Piers—and keep on going—late into the night.

Further, it is very important to identify several individuals, starting in the 1960s, who promoted running, creating races and leading running clubs, etc., and whose names are synonymous with the growth of the sport in the state. They include Rollie Dyer, Dick Goodie, Dale Lincoln, Conrad Walton, Fred Merriam, Gerry St. Amand, Brian Gillespie, Gene Roy, David Paul, Larry Allen, Gary Allen, etc.

Yes, like a number of other extraordinary impacts felt throughout society in Maine and in the United States in the 1960s, the sport of running started with little baby steps and then sped into high gear.

And no one, it can be safely argued, made any more important steps in this development than a young lady, running alone, on a four-and-one-half-mile loop of her summer home in Lamoine.

Afterword

WHEN I SET OUT TO WRITE THIS BOOK I had no idea where it would begin—but not long after my research was completed, including poring over Robin's wonderful scrapbooks, I knew exactly where "The End" of the book was going to come.

Back in 1983, Robin spoke at a high school assembly in Blue Hill, and told the students, staff, and administration of George Stevens Academy she hoped, one day, she would ultimately become "a fast ninety-year-old."

No one who knows her, no one who is familiar with her history, and certainly no one who has just read this book could doubt where Robin hopes her "long and winding road" with long distance running is going to take her. *Long*, indeed, may you run, Robin, Maine's Grand "First Lady" of the Roads.

A final note: I hope, with this manuscript, to raise awareness of an occasionally difficult matter with regard to a woman's identity once she becomes "a public figure," especially where it concerns a name change, as the result of divorce.

I first came to consider the difficulty of all this when a race director from well north of southern Maine approached me with what he felt was a novel idea. He'd studied the times posted by one Kim Beaulieu of Standish in the late 1970s into the mid-1980s and, now, a little later into the 1980s, had contrasted those by one Kim Moody of Portland and felt if he could attract both to his race, he'd have a fine duel for the women's title.

Knowing my friend Kim as well as I did, it allowed me to laugh and tell him that, rest assured, if "you get one, you'll get the other." I then

After running the 2012 Tour du Lac 10-miler with Robin (in the Sub 5 singlet), the author receives his 100 Mile Club certificate. Robin, of course, had hers long before!

revealed to him that Kim had resumed using her birth name following a divorce.

I admit that I was saddened when I looked down the list of women's champions for the Portland Boys Club 5-Mile Race to discover that for her first several victories in Portland Robin was identified as "Voelker" in race records and then, for her final victory, in 1986, she was identified as "Rappa." How unfair it would be for people to NOT immediately recognize that Robin is the all-time women's champion, with nine victories. No other woman is even close.

I'm imploring those entrusted with recordkeeping at this race, and any other race, where Robin is listed under any name other than "Emery" to, please, make the change now. And wherever it is known where women have changed identities, do right by them, now, and make clear that their marriage status should in no way cloud their athletic identities.

Acknowledgments

ROBIN WISHES TO EXPRESS her heartfelt gratitude to Dick "Hogan" Goodie and Jeff Johnson, who believed in her and supported her as she took those first steps onto the competitive racing roads of Maine, and to her dad, Gordon, who accompanied her so many times, to cheer and photograph her.

The author is, first and foremost, grateful to Robin Emery, a true legendary athlete, fellow runner of roads, and longtime friend. Her graciousness in providing ample interviewing time and hosting relaxed, work-session pizza get-togethers at her home in Lamoine were the absolute foundation for the project. She has my heartfelt thanks for her trust and her support. Access to her scrapbooks meant I could see her career through the writings of many outstanding journalists throughout the decades, most notably Bob Haskell of the *Bangor Daily News* and the late Vern Putney of the *Portland Press Herald*. And, of course, the photos she collected and provided for this manuscript significantly enhance the telling of her very special story of fifty years of running the roads of Maine. It is a fitting tribute to her dad, the late Gordon Emery, I believe, to feature photographs of Robin in every era doing what she so loves to do—because her dad took such joy in accompanying his daughter to races and photographing her himself.

There really aren't the words to properly thank my wife, the former Susan Ogilvie of Fredericton, New Brunswick, for her inspiration and her support over the course of this project. One memory of her support will stay with me forever: I had purchased a new computer program, which takes audio tapings and translates them into raw text, saving a writer hours and hours of transcribing interviews. Unfortunately, the relatively new technology requires a number of troublesome and taxing steps to integrate. After a full day of working on my manuscript and then growing completely frustrated with the technology to bring in my latest interview, I left it to Susan at around seven o'clock in the evening. She had spent the entire day at work, as a dental hygienist. I fell asleep—and awakened at just short of 10:00 p.m. to find Susan still struggling to successfully make the program work. She only stopped when I told her how late it was. Yet she was at the computer first thing in the morning, and successfully translated my audio tape into raw text for my use that day before she set off for another full workday. In addition to proofreading the manuscript (she's wonderful for catching grammar and spelling errors), she also helped me properly format the entire manuscript, and scanned and cropped photographs and inserted them into the manuscript so I could experiment with seeing where the artwork for each chapter might best be employed. Yes, her computer skills far exceed those of the author's and her technical support was extraordinary on this project. Thank you, so much, honey! I love you!

I am also grateful to New Brunswick author and former college professor Ron Rees of St. Andrews by the Sea. It was while attending the launch of his latest book, in November of 2016, that Ron's heartfelt words both grabbed and inspired me. He noted how the subject of his biography "deserved to have a book" written about him, and it stabbed me into remembering how many times over the decades I have said Robin Emery "deserves" to have her story told. I owe you, Ron, a lifetime of coffees to accompany our chats on Water Street in downtown St. Andrews.

The author is grateful for the observations forwarded, writings created, or photographs provided by all of the following: Larry Allen, Jon Aretakis, Tom Atwell, Denny Beers, Joan Benoit Samuelson, Bruce Bickford, Judith Blake, Bob Booker, Hugh Bowden, Vance Brown, Michael Carter, Jerry Crasnick, Robert Cunningham, Auggie Favazza, Lloyd Ferriss, Ken Flanders, Diane Fournier, Getty Images, Adam Goode, Dick and Joyce Goodie, Bob Haskell, Bob Hillgrove, Skip Howard, Ryan King, Tom Kirby, Bill Knight, Rick Krause, Joanne Lanin, Allen Lessels, O. J. Logue, Larry Mahoney, Erik McCarthy, Joan Merriam, the late Carlton Mendell, Peter Millard, Jack Milton, Kim Moody, Sarah Mulcahy, Jim Newett, Steve Norton, the late Andy Palmer, Danny Paul, David Paul,

Hank Pfeifle, the late Vern Putney, Ralph Thomas, Taylor Vortherms, Carol Weeks, John Wiggins, and the late Roland Wirths.

Finally, I am especially indebted to Robin, my wife, Susan, and runner-teacher-coach extraordinaire, Danny Paul, for proofreading help on the manuscript.

Any errors of any kind, from factual to grammatical to typos, are, of course, the responsibility of the author.

About the Author

BORN IN BROOKLINE, Massachusetts, Ed Rice grew up in Bangor, Maine, and graduated from Bangor High School. He holds a BA from Northeastern University and an MEd from the University of Southern Maine.

Formerly a reporter for several daily newspapers, including the *Lewiston Daily Sun* and the *Portland Press Herald*, Rice has also been a theater critic and arts commentator for the *Portland Press Herald*, *Maine Sunday Telegram*, the *Maine Times*, and "Maine Things Considered" on MPBN radio. As a military editor with the Maine Army National Guard, he won the Keith L. Ware Award, the Army's top journalism prize, and the Thomas Jefferson Award, the Department of Defense's top journalism prize.

He has taught both college and high school English and journalism and coached

Author runs the 1990 Omaha (Nebraska) Marathon

cross-country. An avid long distance runner who completed 27 marathons (including eight Boston Marathons), with personal bests of 36 minutes, 46 seconds in the 10K and 2 hours, 57 minutes, 55 seconds in the marathon, Rice created Bangor's popular Terry Fox 5K in 1982 and directed the charity event for over twenty years. In 1997 he ran across the state of Massachusetts (162 miles in 7 days) in support of The Angel Fund, a research fund he co-created to help find a cure for ALS. Rice also edited *If They Could Only Hear Me*, a collection of personal essays about the fight against ALS. In 2018, he was elected to the Maine Running Hall of Fame. He lives with his wife, Susan, in St. Andrews, New Brunswick.

WITHDRAWN